ANNUAL UPDATE 201

D0531317

US GOVERNMENT & POLITICS

Anthony J. Bennett

HODDER EDUCATION
AN HACHETTE UK COMPANY

Hodder Education, an Hachette UK company, Blenheim Court, George Street, Banbury, Oxfordshire OX16 5BH

Orders

Bookpoint Ltd, 130 Park Drive, Milton Park, Abingdon, Oxfordshire OX14 4SE
tel: 01235 827827
fax: 01235 400401
e-mail: education@bookpoint.co.uk

Lines are open 9.00 a.m.–5.00 p.m., Monday to Saturday, with a 24-hour message answering service. You can also order through the Hodder Education website: www.hoddereducation.co.uk

ISBN 978-1-4718-6801-6

First printed 2017
Impression number 5 4 3 2 1
Year 2020 2019 2018 2017

Typeset by Integra Software Services Pvt. Ltd., Pondicherry, India

Cover photo: smartboy10/Getty

Printed by CPI Group (UK) Ltd, Croydon, CR0 4YY

Hachette UK's policy is to use papers that are natural, renewable and recyclable products and made from wood grown in sustainable forests. The logging and manufacturing processes are expected to conform to the environmental regulations of the country of origin.

Contents

Chapter 1 Still the 'invisible primary'?   1

The Democratic race ■ The Republican race

Chapter 2 The Democrats: Hillary...eventually   8

Those 'first in the nation' states again ■ On to Super Tuesday and
beyond ■ Clinton's caucus problem — again ■ Why Clinton won the
nomination ■ Conclusions

Chapter 3 The Republicans: Trumped!   17

Pruning a crowded field ■ Trying to stop Trump ■ Why Trump won
the nomination ■ Conclusions

Chapter 4 The conventions: hope trumps fear   31

Why conventions still matter ■ Fear: the Republicans in
Cleveland ■ Hope: the Democrats in Philadelphia ■
The aftermath — convention 'bounce'

Chapter 5 The campaign   44

Trump slumps ■ Trump speaks ■ Clinton frustrated...and
collapsing ■ The first debate ■ The second debate ■ The third
debate ■ What happened in the polls? ■ The October surprise

Chapter 6 The result: an overview   57

Pulling down the Blue Wall ■ The result by numbers ■ The role
of third parties ■ It really was a close call ■ Typical Trump and
Clinton voters

Chapter 7 Why did Trump win?   66

Or why did Clinton lose? ■ Why did Trump win? ■ Conclusion

Chapter 8 The congressional elections: ending divided government?   81

Senate elections ■ House elections ■ The end of divided government?

Chapter 9 The Supreme Court in 2016   86

The Court and affirmative action ■ The Court and abortion ■ The Court
and immigration ■ A summary of the 2015–16 term

Chapter 1

Still the 'invisible primary'?

What you need to know

- 'Invisible primary' is the term used to refer to the events in the year prior to a presidential election, before the actual primaries and caucuses begin.

- It is called 'invisible' because, traditionally, events that occurred during this period could not actually be seen. They occurred, as it were, mostly behind the scenes, out of the eye of the media.

- The important things that a would-be candidate needs to concentrate on during this period are increasing name recognition, raising money and putting together the necessary state-based organisation.

- The media now play an increasingly important role during this period by staging intra-party televised debates between the would-be candidates.

- The candidate leading in opinion polls at the end of the invisible primary often goes on to become that party's presidential nominee, thus enhancing the importance of the invisible primary.

- The term 'invisible primary' first came to prominence as the title of a book by Arthur Hadley, published in 1976.

The Democratic race

The election of 2016 was an entirely open election in that neither the incumbent president nor vice president was running, just like the election of 2008. In 2016, President Obama was term-limited by the Twenty-second Amendment, and on 22 October 2015, Vice President Biden announced that he would not, after all, be a candidate.

Open races tend to attract a large field as there is usually no obvious front-runner. So it was in that sense surprising that the Democratic field was never larger than five candidates, and by the last two months of 2015 amounted to just three candidates — Hillary Clinton, Bernie Sanders and a very distant third in Martin O'Malley, who never got to even 5% in the national polls. Two others — Lincoln Chafee and Jim Webb — pulled out over three months before voting began (see Table 1.1). So why was the Democratic field so small?

Table 1.1 Democratic Party presidential candidates, 2016

Name	Current/last political post	Announced (2015)	Exited (order)
Hillary Clinton	Ex-secretary of state	12 April	
Bernie Sanders	Senator (Vermont)	30 April	12 July 2016 (4)
Martin O'Malley	Ex-governor (Maryland)	30 May	1 February 2016 (3)
Lincoln Chafee	Ex-governor (Rhode Island)	3 June	23 October 2015 (2)
Jim Webb	Ex-senator (Virginia)	2 July	20 October 2015 (1)

The simple answer can be given in two words —Hillary Clinton. Clinton, the former first lady (1993–2001), United States senator (2001–09) and secretary of state (2009–13), had such a huge advantage in terms of name recognition, experience, organisation and money-raising potential that other candidates were frightened away. When Clinton announced her candidacy on 12 April 2015, she was already pretty much the presumptive nominee, and once Joe Biden had publicly foresworn a presidential bid, Clinton's position was presumed to be even more unassailable. In this sense, the Democrats seemed to be choosing their presidential nominee in the same way the Republicans usually do — by picking the person whose turn it seemed to be. As Table 1.2 shows, the Republicans chose as their presidential nominee the runner-up in the previous competitive primaries in five of the six election cycles between 1980 and 2012 when the party has not renominated the incumbent president. As the runner-up in 2008, it seemed that the Democrats were about to adopt the Republicans' strategy. They thought it was Hillary Clinton's turn.

Table 1.2 Republican presidential candidates in open races, 1980–2012

Ronald Reagan	Runner-up in 1976	Nominated in 1980
George H. W. Bush	Runner-up in 1980	Nominated in 1988
Bob Dole	Runner-up in 1992	Nominated in 1996
George W. Bush	*	Nominated in 2000
John McCain	Runner-up in 2000	Nominated in 2008
Mitt Romney	Runner-up in 2008	Nominated in 2012

*Had not previously run in a presidential campaign.

Clinton led the national opinion polls throughout 2015. The trouble is that at this early stage, opinion polls can be as much about name recognition as popularity. Of the five declared candidates, Clinton was the only one with national name recognition after over two decades in national politics. She entered 2015 at 61%, fell to just 40% by the end of September, but picked up to 51.6% by the year's end (see Figure 1.1).

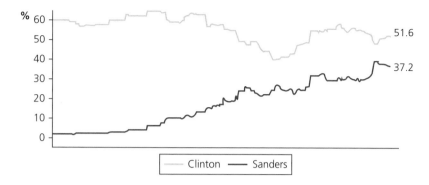

Figure 1.1 Democratic presidential nomination national polls, 2015

Source: www.realclearpolitics.com

But the polls also showed some weaknesses for Clinton. The Gallup poll between mid-September and mid-October found that while Clinton had a net favourability rating of 57% among Democrat women, it was only 43% among Democrat men. Furthermore, the polls in November found that while she enjoyed 66% approval among Democrats aged 65+, this figure fell to just 39% among 18–29-year-olds. Male and younger Democrats preferred Sanders over Clinton. Furthermore, Clinton was not performing all that strongly in the head-to-head polls against potential Republican opponents. Although she was consistently besting Republican front-runner Donald Trump, she was lagging against both Ted Cruz and Marco Rubio.

There were, I think, four reasons why Clinton was not able to see off the Sanders challenge during 2015. First, Democrats hate a coronation. Unlike the Republicans, they genuinely prefer a contest. So, as in 2008, Clinton's 'inevitability' worked against her. Second, Clinton's campaign lacked a focused message. Sure, you knew who Hillary was, but what did she stand for? Third, there was Clinton's wooden campaigning style, which had changed little from her appearances on her husband's campaigns two or three decades ago. But today's audiences want more than the mere parroting of pre-scripted sound bites. In her television debates with Sanders and O'Malley, it was Sanders who looked the more energised. Fourth, as usual with a Clinton campaign, there was the 'S' word — scandal. Maybe the subject matter was different this time — it wasn't money or sex — but the scandal about her State Department e-mails sounded very Clintonesque and the painfully weak excuse lines were all too familiar.

So within the Democratic Party in 2015, can we realistically talk about an 'invisible primary'? The balanced answer is 'yes' and 'no'. Yes we can, in that some of the important political activity during this period was still invisible: fundraising; the gathering of political and media endorsements; the assembling of campaign staffs; the planning for election year itself. But on the other hand, the ubiquitous intra-party television debates and the endless media commentary

and coverage make it difficult to describe anything else during this period of the campaign as invisible. It was all too visible. That said, the Democrats — sensibly in my view — did cut the number of intra-party television debates from 26 in 2007–08 to just six in 2015–16, four of which were to be held before voting began. Sanders and O'Malley were critical of this very significant reduction, claiming it was a ploy by the Democratic National Committee to protect Hillary Clinton's front-runner position. Thus, on the eve of the Iowa caucuses, Clinton was still very definitely the front-runner — no change there — but looked a little more vulnerable than we had expected. It all sounded rather like 2008.

The Republican race

What the Democrats lacked in terms of numbers, the Republicans seemed determined to make up for. By the end of July 2015 they had 17 declared candidates — the largest field ever seen. There were six former governors, four senators, three governors, one former senator, a business CEO (Fiorina), a retired neurosurgeon (Carson) and a star of reality television (Trump) (see Table 1.3). It would be a pre-election year that defied most of the usual rules about who would emerge as the party's front-runner.

Table 1.3 Republican Party presidential candidates, 2016

Name	Current/last political post	Announced (2015)	Exited (order)
Ted Cruz	Senator (Texas)	23 March	3 May 2016 **(15)**
Rand Paul	Senator (Kentucky)	7 April	4 February 2016 **(7)**
Marco Rubio	Senator (Florida)	13 April	15 March 2016 **(14)**
Ben Carson	[none]	3 May	4 March 2016 **(13)**
Carly Fiorina	[none]	4 May	10 February 2016 **(9)**
Mike Huckabee	Ex-governor (Arkansas)	5 May	1 February 2016 **(6)**
Rick Santorum	Ex-senator (Pennsylvania)	27 May	4 February 2016 **(8)**
George Pataki	Ex-governor (New York)	28 May	29 December 2015 **(5)**
Lindsey Graham	Senator (South Carolina)	1 June	21 December 2015 **(4)**
Rick Perry	Ex-governor (Texas)	4 June	11 September 2015 **(1)**
Jeb Bush	Ex-governor (Florida)	15 June	20 February 2016 **(12)**
Donald Trump	[none]	16 June	—
Bobby Jindal	Ex-governor (Louisiana)	24 June	17 November 2015 **(3)**
Chris Christie	Governor (New Jersey)	30 June	10 February 2016 **(10)**
Scott Walker	Governor (Wisconsin)	13 July	21 September 2015 **(2)**
John Kasich	Governor (Ohio)	21 July	4 May 2016 **(16)**
Jim Gilmore	Ex-governor (Virginia)	30 July	12 February 2016 **(11)**

Two days in June encapsulated this bizarre year. On Monday 15 June, a big crowd had assembled at Miami Dade College. It was a culturally diverse crowd and it had come together to witness the declaration by the former Florida governor Jeb Bush that he would be a candidate for the presidency in 2016. Bush had the same advantages that Clinton had — name recognition, experience, organisation and money-raising potential — but it was already clear that these were not going to frighten off other potential candidates. Ten other Republicans had already thrown their hats into the ring. But as the son and brother of former presidents and two-term Florida governor, Bush was the quintessential establishment candidate. He was also the presumptive front-runner — the man to beat. He had the aura of electability. He had gravitas, and his speeches were finely tuned and received rave reviews from the assembled media.

Just 24 hours later another boisterous crowd had gathered — this one in the marble-clad lobby of an iconic skyscraper on Fifth Avenue in Midtown Manhattan in New York City. This was Trump Tower, and down the escalator came the man who built and owns the place — businessman, real-estate developer, property magnate and reality television star Donald Trump. Trump was the ultimate insurgent candidate. He had lots of name recognition and self-made money, but no political experience. His speech appeared almost off the cuff; his language harsh, negative, inflammatory. He went after President Obama, China and illegal immigrants. He claimed that those who were illegally crossing the border into the country from Mexico were drug dealers, rapists and murderers. The crowd loved it, but the speech drew instant criticism from the media and the party establishment. Surely Trump could not be anything more than a footnote in the 2016 Republican presidential race.

But in less than one month, Trump overtook Bush in the polls, and by September Trump was flying high with 30% in a 17-horse race, with Bush back in a distant third place on just 7%. Trump would maintain that front-runner position for the remainder of 2015, ending the year with a 17 percentage-point lead over his nearest rival, and a 31-point lead over Bush, who by this time was back in sixth place with the also-rans. The Republican Party, the deferential party, the party that — as we have already seen — usually nominates its presidential candidates by answering the question 'Whose turn is it?', had become the party of insurgency and grassroots rebellion. The Republican Party had been the subject of a hostile takeover by Mr Trump.

Box 1.1	One year, two races

The year 2015 will be remembered as one of the most bizarrely compelling and genuinely unnerving in the nation's modern political history. It is clear now that there were two halves to the year for the Republican Party: BT and AT, Before Trump and After Trump. From January to mid-June the story of the Republican race was mostly conventional, with Bush the focal point. But those early months were only a prelude to the real events that would follow. It is hardly overstatement to say that on 16 June everything changed — though no-one knew it at the time, not even Trump.

Dan Balz, 'One Year, Two Races: Inside the Republican Party's Bizarre, Tumultuous 2015', *Washington Post*, 3 January 2016

Trump spent the second half of 2015 rewriting the Republican's invisible primary rulebook. The 'rules' said that you couldn't be the front-runner for all those months leading up to Iowa and New Hampshire without having any political or elective experience at all. But Trump had no such experience and yet led from July through December. Conventional wisdom said that you couldn't throw millions of your own money at your nomination bid and not be accused of trying to 'buy' the election, thereby turning off the vast majority of potential supporters. Trump was vulgar and rude about his opponents — and yet his poll numbers kept rising. He was an old-fashioned television-centred candidate in a digital age — and yet he remained the front-runner. He was loathed and despised by the Republican Party establishment — and yet he seemed to be running away with their presidential nomination. And on the other side of the coin, in this most bizarre of years, was the sight of Jeb Bush — the quintessential Republican establishment candidate with zillions of dollars raised, name recognition on steroids, and relevant political experience — languishing in single figures in the polls. It just didn't seem to make any sense at all.

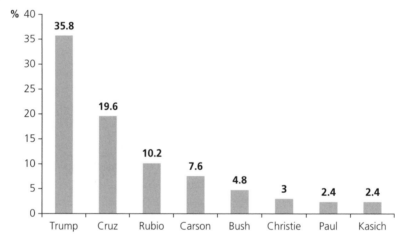

Figure 1.2 Percentage support of leading Republican presidential candidates in national polls, 31 January 2016

Source: www.realclearpolitics.com

Then there were the Republican televised debates. There were so many candidates that the sponsoring media outlets couldn't even fit them all on the same platform. To get around the problem, they started to run two debates. On each designated date there was a secondary, afternoon debate (referred to in uncomplimentary fashion as the 'kids' table') for those in the lower half of the national polls, followed by a main, evening primetime debate for the leading candidates. There were seven such debates in the six months from August 2015 to the start of the primary season on 1 February 2016. In the end, just six candidates — Bush, Carson, Cruz, Kasich, Rubio and Trump — were invited to all seven of the main debates, though Trump chose to boycott the last one. But with the numbers involved, and with Donald Trump mostly involved, these debates turned into a political circus with little if any serious policy debate occurring. As a slightly dejected Ben Carson commented after the debate just four days before voting started:

> This format is not the best format for convincing anybody of anything. We're dealing with sound bites as opposed to being able to explain something in depth. But unfortunately that's characteristic of the society we live in today.

So by the close of the so-called invisible primary, Trump had a 16-point lead over his nearest rival — Senator Ted Cruz of Texas (see Figure 1.2), another anti-establishment candidate. Add in another anti-establishment candidate in retired neurosurgeon Ben Carson and these three commanded 63% of the vote in what was still a 12-horse race. Or to put it another way, the remaining nine establishment candidates had to divide the remaining 37% between them. That didn't leave much to go round and left the Republican Party establishment with a huge problem on the eve of the Iowa caucuses. An invisible primary? Some of us were quietly wishing it had been.

Questions

1 What is an 'open' election or race?
2 Why did the emergence of Hillary Clinton as the Democratic front-runner in some ways resemble the way Republican front-runners usually emerge?
3 What four reasons are given for Clinton's inability to see off the challenge from Bernie Sanders in 2015?
4 What were the differences between the Jeb Bush and Donald Trump events in June 2015?
5 In what ways did Trump's campaign 'rewrite the Republicans' rulebook'?
6 What problems surrounded the Republican candidate debates?
7 How did 2015 end for Clinton and Trump?

Chapter 2

The Democrats: Hillary...eventually

What you need to know

- Presidential primaries are state-based elections held between February and June of the presidential election year.
- They give ordinary voters a chance to say whom they would like to be their party's candidate in the upcoming presidential election.
- Voters in the primaries also choose delegates to go to the national party conventions held in late summer, which is where the final decision about the candidate is made.
- Some small, sparsely populated states hold caucuses rather than a primary.
- Caucuses are a series of meetings held across the state which perform the same functions as primaries.

Those 'first in the nation' states again

Back in 2008, Hillary Clinton was ambushed in Iowa. The undisputed front-runner when the voting began, she finished third in the Iowa caucuses. And although she eked out a three-point win in New Hampshire five days later, she was already damaged goods. This year it was sort of different, but hardly more successful. When Iowa Democrats went to the caucuses on 1 February, Clinton came out on top this time, but by the narrowest of margins. The popular vote was not declared, but in terms of state party convention delegates, Clinton won 49.9% to 49.6% for Sanders.

Table 2.1 Margins of victory in contested Democratic New Hampshire primaries, 1968–2016

Rank	Year	Percentage-point win	Winner	Runner-up
1	2016	22.4	Bernie Sanders	**Hillary Clinton**
2	1988	16.0	**Michael Dukakis**	Dick Gephardt
3	2004	12.1	**John Kerry**	Howard Dean
4	1980	9.8	**Jimmy Carter**	Edward Kennedy
5	1984	9.4	Gary Hart	**Walter Mondale**
6	1972	9.2	Ed Muskie	**George McGovern**
7	1992	8.4	Paul Tsongas	**Bill Clinton**
8	1968	7.7	Lyndon Johnson	Eugene McCarthy
9	1976	5.7	**Jimmy Carter**	Morris Udall
10	2000	4.1	**Al Gore**	Bill Bradley
11	2008	2.6	Hillary Clinton	**Barack Obama**

Bold: eventual candidates

But eight days later, Clinton lost by a huge 22 percentage points to Sanders in the New Hampshire primary. Now true, Sanders is the senator from neighbouring Vermont, but 22 points! This was the biggest winning margin in a contested New Hampshire Democratic presidential primary throughout the entire history of the modern primary era, beating the 16-point victory of Michael Dukakis over Dick Gephardt back in 1988 (see Table 2.1).

What was more, the exit polls showed up some alarming weaknesses in the Clinton appeal. Only 44% of women voted for Clinton; 55% voted for Sanders. She attracted only 25% of those earning less than $30,000 year. Those aged 18–29 gave Clinton only 16% of their votes. Of the 34% of voters who said that being 'honest and trustworthy' was the most important candidate quality — the single quality named by most voters — 92% voted for Sanders, and just 6% for Clinton. Clinton clearly had problems among key groups of voters.

On to Super Tuesday and beyond

But Clinton recovered, and won comfortable victories in both Nevada and South Carolina — the two other states to vote in February. She also emerged as the clear winner on Super Tuesday, winning 7 of the 11 contests, while Sanders' only primary wins were in Oklahoma and his home state of Vermont, along with caucus wins in Colorado and Minnesota. In terms of delegates, she won 519 compared to 359 for Sanders.

Clinton had another big win two weeks later (15 March), winning all five contests that day — in Florida, Illinois, Missouri, North Carolina and Ohio — though her victory margins in Illinois and Missouri were wafer thin. But then between 22 March and 9 April, Sanders won 7 out 8 of contests. However, these were mostly in small, caucus states — Idaho, Utah, Alaska, Hawaii, Washington and Wyoming. But on 5 April, Sanders beat Clinton 56–43 in the Wisconsin primary, another big blow to the former first lady's bandwagon. Then on the last two Tuesdays of April, the pendulum swung back in Clinton's favour with 5 wins out of 6, including a 16-point win in New York. But she never seemed to be able to seal the deal and see off Sanders.

Although in the end the outcome was as expected, the manner in which Clinton won her glass ceiling-breaking victory told us quite a bit about both her vulnerabilities and weaknesses as well as about the durability and tenacity of Bernie Sanders. Sanders was never going to win the nomination, but that he managed to push her as close as he did and for as long as he did was a significant achievement. And the over 1,800 delegates that he won to the national convention gave him the policy clout that he wanted. In the end Clinton won the contests in 28 states plus the District of Columbia, with Sanders winning in 22. Clinton won 56% of the popular vote to 43% for Sanders.

Table 2.2 Democratic Party primary/caucus results, 2016

Date	State	Clinton (%)	Sanders (%)
1 **February**	Iowa (C)	**49.9**	49.6
9 February	New Hampshire	38	**60**
20 February	Nevada (C)	**53**	47
27 February	South Carolina	**74**	26
1 **March**	Alabama	**78**	19
	Arkansas	**66**	30
	Colorado (C)	40	**59**
	Georgia	**71**	28
	Massachusetts	**50**	49
	Minnesota (C)	38	**62**
	Oklahoma	42	**52**
	Tennessee	**66**	32
	Texas	**65**	33
	Vermont	14	**86**
	Virginia	**64**	35
5 March	Kansas (C)	32	**68**
	Louisiana	**71**	23
	Nebraska (C)	44	**56**
6 March	Maine (C)	35	**64**
8 March	Michigan	48	**50**
	Mississippi	**83**	17
15 March	Florida	**64**	33
	Illinois	**50**	49
	Missouri	**50**	49
	North Carolina	**55**	41
	Ohio	**57**	43
22 March	Arizona	**58**	40
	Idaho (C)	21	**78**
	Utah (C)	20	**80**
26 March	Alaska (C)	18	**82**
	Hawaii (C)	30	**70**
	Washington (C)	27	**73**
5 **April**	Wisconsin	43	**56**
9 April	Wyoming (C)	44	**56**
19 April	New York	**58**	42

Date	State	Clinton (%)	Sanders (%)
26 April	Connecticut	**52**	47
	Delaware	**60**	39
	Maryland	**63**	33
	Pennsylvania	**56**	44
	Rhode Island	43	**55**
3 **May**	Indiana	47	**52**
10 May	West Virginia	36	**52**
17 May	Kentucky	**47**	46
	Oregon	44	**56**
7 **June**	California	**55**	44
	Montana	44	**51**
	New Jersey	**63**	37
	New Mexico	**51**	48
	North Dakota (C)	27	**64**
	South Dakota	**51**	49
14 June	District of Columbia	**78**	21

Winner in bold C = caucuses

Clinton's caucus problem — again

When Hillary Clinton ran for the party's presidential nomination in 2008, one of the reasons she lost was her dismal performance in those 13 states that held caucuses rather than a primary. She lost all but one of those contests, winning just 142 delegates to Obama's 283, and winning only 33% of the vote. Her performance in caucus states was equally poor this time around. This time she managed to win in the caucuses in Iowa, by a whisker, and also won in Nevada — the one caucus state she won in 2008. Those were also the first two states to hold caucuses. She then lost the remaining 12, winning just 184 delegates to 333 for Sanders, and winning just over 35% of the vote.

It is a general rule of thumb in both parties that insurgent candidates — such as Bernie Sanders — tend to do much better in caucuses than do establishment candidates like Clinton. This is because turnout in caucuses tends to be much lower than in primaries, and those who turn out in caucuses tend to be the more politically active and ideological. This raises once again the question of the place of caucuses in the presidential nomination contest.

Why Clinton won the nomination

So what circumstances and factors contributed to Hillary Clinton becoming the first female presidential candidate of a major party? Let's consider four of the main factors that led to Clinton's victory.

The delegate selection process

The first reason for Hillary Clinton's victory in the Democratic primaries was the way delegates are allocated in the Democratic Party. Although the vast majority of delegates are chosen in primaries or caucuses, around 15% are so-called super delegates — professional party office holders who have automatic places at the Democratic Convention and are selected as uncommitted delegates (see Box 2.1). Super delegates first appeared back in 1984 in an attempt to include some level of 'peer review' to the candidate selection process.

Box 2.1 Make-up of the 2016 super delegates

- 438 members of the Democratic National Committee (DNC)
- 20 'distinguished party leaders' (former presidents and vice presidents, former DNC chairs and congressional leaders)
- 193 Democratic members of the House of Representatives
- 47 Democratic members of the Senate
- 21 Democratic state governors

Back in 2008, this group had initially lined up with Hillary Clinton, but as Senator Obama won more and more primaries, gradually they switched their allegiance to him. This was one of the main reasons why Clinton lost the 2008 nomination.

This year, it was all quite different. In terms of pledged delegates won in the primaries, Clinton won 55% to 45% for Sanders, a mirror of the popular vote divide between the two candidates. But it was Clinton's sweep of the super delegates, of which she won over 90%, that eventually secured her the 2,382 delegate votes required for the first ballot victory at the convention.

This time, her experience was an asset

When Hillary Clinton ran for the presidential nomination in 2008, she advertised her political experience as one of her greatest assets. It was something the exit polls showed she beat Barack Obama on in every primary. The trouble was that 'experience' was not what Democratic primary voters were looking for eight years ago. They wanted 'change'.

But fast forward to 2016 and it was all very different, as Table 2.3 clearly shows. In selected primaries, well over three-quarters of Democratic primary voters were now saying that what they wanted in their candidate was 'political experience', and among those who were saying that, Clinton easily beat Sanders in most states. In some states this might have been the decisive factor in Clinton's victory. In Illinois, for example, 82% of voters said they wanted an 'experienced' candidate, and of that 82%, 56% voted for Clinton and just 43% for Sanders. Clinton won the primary by just 1 percentage point. The figures were almost identical in Missouri, where again Clinton was the winner by a wafer-thin margin.

Table 2.3 Results from selected primaries
Q: Should the next president be experienced in politics or outside the establishment?

State	Percentage wanting candidate 'experienced in politics'	Vote for Clinton (%)	Vote for Sanders (%)
New Hampshire	70	50	50
South Carolina	85	82	18
Georgia	86	76	24
Illinois	82	56	43
Missouri	80	58	42
Virginia	84	71	29
Ohio	81	61	38
Wisconsin	77	51	48
Texas	82	75	24

The weakness of the Democratic field

As in 2008, Hillary Clinton had the advantage of a thin and weak field. Indeed, the field in 2016 must be regarded as one of the thinnest in terms of both number and political stature for many decades, consisting as it did of two former governors of small Mid-Atlantic states, a one-term senator from Virginia who had served in a *Republican* administration, and a slightly whacky 74-year-old ex-socialist from Vermont. And then there was Hillary Clinton — the former first lady, United States senator and secretary of state. By the time of the New Hampshire primary, the race had only two contestants — Hillary and Bernie.

The marvel was that Hillary Clinton struggled so hard and for so long to see off her septuagenarian opponent and lost 18 of the first 40 primaries and caucuses to him, some of them by colossal margins. Her defeats in Michigan (8 March), Wisconsin (5 April) and Indiana (3 May) were particularly bewildering. She had, for example, beaten Obama in Indiana back in 2008, and now she was losing it to Sanders in 2016, and by 5 percentage points.

How different things might have been had other Democratic Party big names thrown their hats into the ring, the likes of: Governor Andrew Cuomo of New York, Senator Amy Klobuchar of Minnesota, Governor Deval Patrick and Senator Elizabeth Warren of Massachusetts, Senator Mark Warner of Virginia, or Vice President Joe Biden. But for a host of reasons — and maybe largely because they thought 2016 would not be a strong year for Democrats, or they were scared off by the Clinton name — none of these showed up at the races. That was a huge relief to Hillary Clinton.

Her policies were more in line with the majority of Democratic primary voters

Certainly there were significant policy differences between Hillary Clinton and Bernie Sanders (see Table 2.4).

Table 2.4 Selected policy differences between Clinton and Sanders at the beginning of the Democratic primaries

Policy area	Clinton's policy	Sanders' policy
Federal minimum wage	Supported raising it to $12 an hour	Supported raising it to $15 an hour
Immigration reform	Supported enforcing Obama's executive actions	Supported expanding Obama's executive actions
Climate change	Proposed renewable energy to account for one-third of all energy produced in USA by 2027	Proposed eliminating tax breaks for fossil-fuel companies
Healthcare	Supported leaving Obamacare in place	Supported replacing Obamacare with single-payer healthcare system
Gun control	Has supported legislation that allows victims of gun violence to sue manufacturers	Has opposed legislation that allows victims of gun violence to sue manufacturers
College affordability	Proposed giving $17.5 billion in grants to states to invest in higher education	Proposed making tuition in all public colleges cost free by taxing Wall Street
Drugs	Proposed rescheduling marijuana to a lower drug classification	Supported states' rights to legalise marijuana without federal intervention
Training Syrian rebels to fight ISIS	Supported it	Opposed it
Afghanistan	Open to maintaining some US troops there if necessary	Called for withdrawal of all US troops

As the primary season played out, Clinton was prepared to move towards Sanders on some issues. So for example, although she did not wholeheartedly endorse Sanders' call for a $15 an hour federal minimum wage, she did say that as president she would not veto it. The Democratic Party hierarchy also moved towards Sanders on drug policy, Wall Street reform and the death penalty. But in the end it was Clinton who had the policies that appealed to the majority of the Democratic voters.

Exit polls also showed up that Clinton and Sanders voters were both looking for different strengths and qualities in their candidate, and took different positions on policy areas such as the economy, trade and Wall Street (see Table 2.5). In the end, more Democratic primary voters thought that the economy and jobs mattered more than income inequality, that on balance trade created more jobs in the USA, that Wall Street helps more than it hurts, and that experience and winning mattered more than honesty and empathy.

Table 2.5 Policy and candidate quality differences between Clinton and Sanders voters

Issue	Clinton voters	Sanders voters
Issue that mattered most	Economy/jobs	Income inequality
Direction of the nation's economy	Somewhat worried about it	Very worried about it
Trade with other countries	Creates more jobs in the USA	Takes away jobs from the USA
Effect of Wall Street	Helps the US economy	Hurts the US economy
Next president's policies	Should be the same as Obama's	Should be more liberal than Obama's
Most important candidate qualities	Has the right experience; can win in November	Honest and trustworthy; cares about people like me

It was also possible, therefore, to discern clear differences between typical Clinton voters and typical Sanders voters (see Table 2.6). Her voters were more likely to be older, white or non-white, wealthier married women. His voters were more likely to be younger, white, less wealthy, single men who were participating in the Democratic primaries for the first time.

Table 2.6 Typical Clinton and Sanders voters

Typical Clinton voters	Typical Sanders voters
• women	• men
• older	• young
• non-white	• white
• more wealthy	• poorer
• married	• single
	• first-time voters

Conclusions

It was perhaps something of an irony that when the official confirmation came that Hillary Clinton had become the first woman in America to secure the presidential nomination of a major party, it came not as a result of the votes of real people in a primary, but in an announcement by the Associated Press news agency on 6 June, the day before the last big swathe of primaries. Indeed, its announcement was made only after it had received private indications as to how the super delegates would vote, for Clinton was still some hundreds of votes short of the required majority in terms of pledged delegates chosen in the primaries.

It was all a bit of a damp squib. It was Hillary — eventually, after over eight years of trying. Hillary Clinton has been on the national stage for almost a quarter of a century. She has served as first lady, United States senator and secretary of state. She has twice contested the Democratic Party's presidential nomination — first losing narrowly, and now winning narrowly. Yet both contests had been against comparatively weak and inexperienced opposition.

Indeed, one could say that the story of the 2016 Democratic primaries had really been dominated by Sanders, not Clinton. It was Sanders who had electrified audiences, which were often larger than Clinton's. They were certainly younger and noisier. It was Sanders who had dominated the policy agenda, forcing Clinton to move to the left in some areas. The real surprise was not that Clinton — the first woman — won, but that Sanders won 22 contests, 43% of the popular vote and over 1,800 delegates. Clinton therefore went forward to the Democratic convention as a victorious but vulnerable candidate against a highly unpredictable Republican opponent.

Questions

1 Using the data in Table 2.1 and the exit poll data quoted in the text, explain what happened in the New Hampshire primary.
2 What happened on Super Tuesday?
3 How did Clinton perform in the states that held caucuses. Why was this?
4 Explain who the super delegates are and the role they played in 2016.
5 What were the main factors that led Clinton to win the nomination?
6 How did Clinton and Sanders differ in terms of policy and appeal?

Chapter 3

The Republicans: Trumped!

As winter turned to spring and the Republican primaries became an endless record of the rise of Donald Trump, a social media hash-tag was being talked about — #NeverTrump. This had become the rallying cry of those Republicans who said they could never support Donald Trump, even if he were to become the Republican presidential nominee. But if the same hash-tag had been used just six months earlier, it would probably have been used by those countless political commentators, journalists, pundits, politicians — and yes, even this author — who were telling anyone who cared to listen that Trump could 'never' become the Republican presidential candidate in 2016. How wrong we were. So this chapter needs to explain two things: how it happened, and why it happened.

Pruning a crowded field

By the time the real voting got under way with the Iowa caucuses on 1 February, 12 of the original 17 Republican candidates were still in the race. So dividing the share of the vote among so many candidates was always going to mean a low winning score and a tight winning margin. Texas senator Ted Cruz came home first with just 27% of the vote, with Donald Trump (24%) and Marco Rubio (23%) tight on his heels. The full results showed that most of the votes were going to the non-establishment, insurgent candidates. Cruz, Trump, Ben Carson and Rand Paul — all in their own way political outsiders — scooped up two-thirds of the votes. By contrast, establishment Republicans and Washington insiders struggled to make any headway in the contest at all. Jeb Bush polled 2.8% and John Kasich just 1.9%, finishing in sixth and eighth places respectively. Iowa further thinned the field, leading to the demise of Mike Huckabee, Rand Paul and Rick Santorum. Then there were nine.

So yet again, the winner of the Iowa Republican caucuses was not the party's eventual nominee. For all the hoopla made about them every four years, of the eight contested Iowa Republican caucuses, on only three occasions has the winner gone on to become the party's presidential candidate — in 1976 (Gerald Ford), in 1996 (Bob Dole) and in 2000 (George W. Bush). None of the past three winners — Mike Huckabee (2008), Rick Santorum (2012) and now Ted Cruz (2016) — has gone on to win the nomination.

In New Hampshire, Trump had led in the polls for over six months and in the eve-of-primary poll he held a 17 percentage-point lead over his nearest rival, Marco Rubio. Trump's victory when it came was therefore not unexpected. We often comment that primaries, especially early on, are all about expectations — where a candidate exceeds expectations or fails to reach them. One candidate who exceeded expectations in New Hampshire was Governor John Kasich of Ohio, who finished in second place with 16%. Two who underperformed were Rubio who finished fifth and Governor Chris Christie from New Jersey in sixth place. Christie immediately exited the race, as did Carly Fiorina and Jim Gilmore. Then there were just six.

As the contest moved to the south, it was D-Day for former Florida governor Jeb Bush in the South Carolina primary on 20 February. Before Donald Trump's meteoric rise in the Republican race, Jeb Bush — son of a former president and brother of another — was to most people the man to beat. He had everything — experience, name recognition, organisation and, above all, money. By mid-February Bush had raised a staggering $162 million, far exceeding any other Republican candidate. But for all this money, Bush had so far amassed just 36,000 votes and four delegates. When in South Carolina he finished a very distant fourth with just 7% of the vote, Bush packed his bags and left the race. Those four Bush delegates could have been some of the most expensive delegates in presidential nominating history, for they cost around $40 million each! In contrast, Trump was spending just less than $5 per delegate. Bush's exit left just five candidates standing — Carson, Rubio, Cruz, Kasich and Trump.

Box 3.1 Some of Trump's early controversial (and mostly printable) statements

- 'When Mexico sends its people [to America], they're not sending their best. They're sending people that have lots of problems, and they're bringing those with them. They're bringing drugs. They're bring crime. They're rapists. And some, I assume, are good people.' (26 June 2015)
- '[Senator John] McCain is not a war hero, because he was captured. I like people who weren't captured.' (18 July)
- 'Look at that face. Would anyone vote for that? Can you imagine that, the face of our next president? I mean, she's a woman, and I'm not supposed to say bad things, but really folks, come on. Are we serious?' (Talking to a reporter about Republican presidential candidate Carly Fiorina, 9 September)
- 'Donald J. Trump is calling for a complete and total shutdown on Muslims entering the United States until our country's representatives can figure out what the hell is going on.' (Press statement, 7 December)
- 'So if you see somebody getting ready to throw a tomato, knock the c**p out of 'em, would you? Seriously. Okay? Just knock the hell — I promise you I will pay for the legal fees. I promise. I promise.' (Addressing rally in Cedar Rapids, Iowa, 1 February 2016)

Even with such a pruned and weakened field, it still seemed quite impossible that Trump could win the nomination. He was just too much of a loose cannon as a selection of his comments early in the campaign clearly shows (see Box 3.1). And as February closed, Trump had created another rumpus by refusing to denounce the endorsement given to him by the white supremacist leader and former Grand Wizard of the Ku Klux Klan, David Duke. Surely someone who insulted immigrants, war heroes, women, religious minorities and indeed any of his opponents, and who advocated violence with the use of openly vulgar language — surely they would not be deemed fit to hold the highest office in the land?

Table 3.1 Republican Party primary/caucus results, 2016

Date	State	Cruz (%)	Kasich (%)	Rubio (%)	Trump (%)
1 **February**	Iowa (C)	**27**	2	23	24
9 February	New Hampshire	12	16	10	**35**
20 February	South Carolina	22	7	23	**32**
23 February	Nevada (C)	21	4	24	**46**
1 **March**	Alabama	21	4	19	**43**
	Alaska (C)	**36**	4	15	34
	Arkansas	30	4	25	**33**
	Georgia	24	6	24	**39**
	Massachusetts	10	18	10	**49**
	Minnesota (C)	29	6	**37**	21
	Oklahoma	**34**	4	26	28
	Tennessee	25	5	21	**39**
	Texas	**44**	4	18	27
	Vermont	10	30	19	**33**
	Virginia	17	9	32	**35**
5 March	Kansas (C)	**48**	11	17	23
	Kentucky (C)	32	14	16	**36**
	Louisiana	38	6	11	**41**
	Maine (C)	**46**	12	8	33
8 March	Hawaii (C)	33	11	13	**42**
	Idaho (C)	**45**	7	16	28
	Michigan	25	24	9	**37**
	Mississippi	36	9	5	**47**
12 March	District of Columbia (C)	12	35	**37**	14
15 March	Florida	17	7	27	**46**
	Illinois	30	20	9	**39**
	Missouri	41	10	6	**41**
	North Carolina	37	13	8	**40**
	Ohio	13	**47**	3	36
22 March	Arizona	25	10	–	**47**
	Utah (C)	**69**	17	–	14

Date	State	Cruz (%)	Kasich (%)	Rubio (%)	Trump (%)
1–3 **April**	North Dakota (SC)	Elected slate of uncommitted delegates			
5 April	Wisconsin	48	14	–	35
9 April	Colorado (SC)	**Won**	–	–	–
16 April	Wyoming (SC)	**Won**	–	–	–
19 April	New York	14	25	–	60
26 April	Connecticut	12	29	–	58
	Delaware	16	20	–	61
	Maryland	19	23	–	54
	Pennsylvania	22	19	–	57
	Rhode Island	10	24	–	64
3 **May**	Indiana	37	8	–	53
10 May	Nebraska	18	11	–	61
	West Virginia	9	7	–	77
17 May	Oregon	17	16	–	67
24 May	Washington	11	10	–	76
7 **June**	California	9	11	–	75
	Montana	9	7	–	74
	New Jersey	6	13	–	81
	New Mexico	13	7	–	71
	South Dakota	17	16	–	67

Winner in bold   C = caucuses   SC = state party convention

Trying to stop Trump

In the Republicans' Super Tuesday on 1 March there were 11 contests and some 579 delegates to be chosen — getting on for half of the 1,237 required for the nomination. Of these 11 contests, Trump won seven, with three for Cruz and just one for Rubio. It was at this point that Ben Carson dropped out of the race. Although Trump made a strong showing, with Cruz winning 104 of the 155 delegates from his home state of Texas, Trump was still finding it difficult to rack up the number of delegates he needed. He still feared that, although he might win more delegates than any other Republican, his rivals would prevent him from getting the necessary absolute majority and then deny him the nomination in a **brokered convention**.

A **brokered convention** is a national party convention at the start of which no candidate has the absolute majority of delegate votes necessary to secure the nomination on the first ballot. In subsequent ballots, deals are made (brokered) as delegates switch their support to other candidates until one candidate emerges as the winner. With the increased number of committed delegates chosen in the primaries, brokered conventions have become a thing of the past — the last being the Democratic convention in 1952.

This scenario was given extra impetus when Trump won only 60 of the 152 delegates available in the four contests on 5 March. But Trump fought back to deliver a strong showing in the 15 March contests, including an emphatic win in Florida — a humiliation for Marco Rubio that marked the end to his challenge. On the other hand, John Kasich did win his home state of Ohio and so it was Cruz, Kasich and Trump who remained in the race.

The next month — from mid-March to mid-April — was the moment when the anti-Trump forces almost prevailed. Trump won only one of the six contests held during this period, while Ted Cruz secured four straight wins — in Utah, Wisconsin, Colorado and Wyoming. Indeed, Cruz's easy win over Trump in Wisconsin was seen by many as the turning point we had all been waiting for — the moment when the Trump balloon would deflate. For despite the significant victories Trump had certainly enjoyed, he seemed unable to expand his pool of support. Back on 9 February, Trump had won New Hampshire in a race with 12 candidates with 35% of the vote. Now in Wisconsin, two months later, he had lost a race with just three candidates with, again, 35% of the vote. By contrast, Cruz had grown his share of the vote from 12% in New Hampshire to 48% in Wisconsin. Furthermore, in all the 20 contests that Trump had won, he had yet to gain 50% of the votes in any of them.

These were the weeks when the media started talking up the possibility of there being a brokered Republican convention. The possible scenario went something like this. Trump would arrive at the convention in Cincinnati in July with the most delegates, but without the 1,237 needed for a first ballot victory. On subsequent ballots, Trump delegates would then desert their candidate in favour of either Cruz or Kasich, or possibly even some other compromise candidate such as House Speaker Paul Ryan or the party's 2012 presidential nominee, Mitt Romney. Indeed, Ted Cruz's team were openly approaching Trump delegates to get them to commit to voting for their candidate on the second ballot.

But the events during just eight days in the second half of April pretty much dispelled all such talk. Trump won six straight primaries, including the two big states of New York and Pennsylvania, and won them by overwhelming majorities. The Indiana primary on 3 May was critical for both Cruz and Kasich. If one of them could stop Trump then maybe they could still deny him a first ballot victory at the convention. Indiana was said to be similar to Wisconsin, where Trump had stumbled badly a month earlier. But it was all to no avail. Trump won Indiana by 18 percentage points over Cruz and both he and Kasich folded their campaigns. Trump had achieved the unthinkable. He was now the party's presumptive presidential nominee — a man with no political experience, no national organisation, very little money raised and, according to some, nothing in the way of a thought-through policy agenda.

Table 3.2 Who won the votes and delegates

Candidate	Popular vote	Popular vote (%)	Delegates	Delegates (%)
Donald Trump	14,009,098	45.0	1,441	58.3
Ted Cruz	7,810,477	25.1	551	22.3
John Kasich	4,287,325	13.8	161	6.5
Marco Rubio	3,513,879	11.3	173	7.0
Ben Carson	857,023	2.7	9	0.4
Jeb Bush	286,634	0.9	4	0.2
Rand Paul	66,790	0.2	1	0.04
Mike Huckabee	51,441	0.2	1	0.04
Carly Fiorina	40,578	0.1	1	0.04
Other candidates	166,420	0.2	3	0.1
Uncommitted	70,438	0.2	130	5.3

Of the 37 states that held primaries — as opposed to caucuses or state conventions — Trump won 33 of them. The remaining four were accounted for by Cruz and Kasich each winning their home state primaries of Texas and Ohio respectively, and Cruz's victories in Oklahoma and Wisconsin. Because of the way the Republicans allocate their delegates — many states using either a strict or variant winner-take-all system — Trump was able to win 58% of the delegates on just 45% of the popular vote (see Table 3.2). Kasich and Rubio, on the other hand, who together won 25% of the votes, won just 13% of the delegates. Come June, and Trump liked to remind his audiences that the over 14 million votes he had won were more votes than any other candidate in a Republican nomination contest. While that was true, it was also true that no other candidate had had 17 million votes cast against him. It was also true that his 14 million votes constituted less than a quarter of the number of votes that Republican Mitt Romney had received in November 2012 in losing to President Obama. Trump had a lot of work to do in broadening his voter appeal.

But 16 other Republicans had begun this race, and one by one they had been forced to withdraw. In a word, they had been Trumped. So why did Trump pull off one of the most extraordinary — if not *the* most extraordinary — and most unlikely victories in a presidential nomination contest of either party?

Why Trump won the nomination

Political scientists, journalists and commentators will analyse this cycle of Republican primaries for decades to come. I suspect there will be as many different views on why Trump won as there are books and articles written. But writing soon after these tumultuous events concluded, I venture to suggest three important reasons that go some way to explaining why Trump won the nomination.

The pop culture icon

Trump had flirted with running for the presidency before and those suggestions had been met with almost universal ridicule by those who are well paid to forecast the ups and downs of American politics. This time was no different. Many dismissed Trump's candidacy as a joke. Within the year, all Trump's Republican rivals knew it was no joke. What they also knew was that they, like so many others, had underestimated Trump. They had failed to see that someone who had sustained himself as a highly marketable pop culture icon for more than three decades might make them look too much like the grey, lack-lustre career politicians that most of them were.

Donald Trump's portfolio is quite wide ranging. It extends from real estate to food and wine, from golf to gambling, from buildings to boxing. Trump has been in the media spotlight for decades, whether appearing in Hollywood films or episodes of well-known television sitcoms, promoting football, boxing and World Wrestling Entertainment, hosting beauty pageants, and from 2004 to 2015 producing and starring in the American version of *The Apprentice*, a programme that has regularly attracted between 15 and 20 million viewers for each episode. Trump may not have many of the traditional experiences and qualities of a presidential candidate, but he is the master of television, plays the tabloid media like a fiddle, has listened to decades of conservative talk radio so knows what its listeners want to hear, is the consummate player of social media, and even has his star in the Hollywood Walk of Fame in LA. If you thought that John F. Kennedy and Ronald Reagan were the 'made for television' candidates in an era when network television was king, then Donald Trump is the perfect candidate for today's partisan, social media, sound-bite age. Trump's elevation to major party presidential candidate tells you a lot about America in the second decade of the twenty-first century.

Republican voters' profound disillusionment

This was most critical factor, for if Republican voters had not been so deeply disillusioned by their leaders — in Washington and in the states — Trump would have remained the fringe candidate most expected him to be and would have dropped out of the race after Super Tuesday, if not before. He would have been a footnote, not a phoenix. But aided by some prominent conservative media figures such as Rush Limbaugh and Sean Hannity, Trump was able to present himself as the heir apparent of the Tea Party movement, which many grassroots Republicans felt had been betrayed and killed off by the party establishment — people like Jeb Bush and the Republican leadership in Congress.

Table 3.3 Exit poll data from selected Republican primaries

Q: Do you feel betrayed by Republican politicians?

State	Percentage of Republican primary voters who felt betrayed by Republican politicians	Percentage of those who voted for Trump	Winner of primary
New Hampshire	47	36	Trump
South Carolina	52	36	Trump
Alabama	51	44	Trump
Georgia	54	38	Trump
Tennessee	58	41	Trump
Michigan	58	41	Trump
Florida	60	54	Trump
North Carolina	56	44	Trump
West Virginia	48	75	Trump

Table 3.4 Exit poll data from selected Republican primaries

Q: What are your feelings about the federal government: enthusiastic, satisfied, dissatisfied, angry?

State	Percentage dissatisfied/angry with federal government	Percentage of those who voted for Trump
New Hampshire	88	37
South Carolina	92	33
Alabama	84	46
Georgia	91	40
Tennessee	92	41
Michigan	87	37
Florida	85	49
North Carolina	94	40
West Virginia	92	78

By analysing the exit poll data from Republican primaries, one can see that the most significant determinant of people's attitude to Trump came in answer to two questions. The first was 'Do you feel betrayed by Republican politicians?' In many states over half of the voters in the Republican primary felt betrayed by their own party's politicians. And as most of Trump's rivals were from this group — folk such as Bush, Rubio, Kasich and Perry — this was fertile ground for a Trump campaign (see Table 3.3). In the crucial Florida primary on 15 March, for example, 60% of voters said that Republican politicians had betrayed them. Of that 60%, 54% voted for Trump, while only 18% voted their home-state senator, Marco Rubio.

The second question was 'What are your feelings about the federal government: enthusiastic, satisfied, dissatisfied or angry?' As Table 3.4 shows, the percentage of Republican voters in the latter two categories was alarmingly high, with between 84% and 94% saying they were either dissatisfied or angry. And here was another pool of recruitment for Trump. Even in an 11-candidate race in New Hampshire, Trump received the votes of 37% of the 88% of dissatisfied/angry voters. His nearest rival among these voters was John Kasich with just 16%. It was this profound disaffection with ordinary Republican politicians and sustained dissatisfaction and anger at the federal government that provided the ingredients for a Trump candidacy. Many Republicans felt alienated by their party, their government, even by their country, in which they now felt strangers. In effect, Trump built what could best be described as a 'coalition of resentment'.

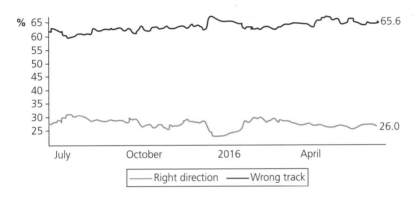

Figure 3.1 Right track/wrong track polling, June 2015–June 2016

Source: www.realclearpolitics.com

We need to make one further related point. Contented countries do not produce politicians such as Donald Trump. In America, pollsters regularly ask the following question: 'In general, do you think things in the nation are headed in the right direction, or have they gotten off on the wrong track?' It's often referred to in short-hand as the right track/wrong track question. For many years now, a majority of Americans have told pollsters — both at elections and between them — that they believe the nation is on 'the wrong track'. This was certainly true in the year following Donald Trump announcing his candidacy in mid-2015, through the primaries and caucuses of 2016 (see Figure 3.1). During this year-long period, those saying the country was on the right track ranged from a high of 31% to a low of 23%, while those saying the country was on the wrong track ranged from a low of 59% to a high of 67%. That is more than two-thirds of voters saying the country is off the rails. As John Cassidy commented in a piece in *The New Yorker* in May 2016, 'A decade-and-a-half marked by foreign wars, terrorist threats, recession, slow growth, political gridlock, culture wars and (for many voters) declining incomes have further undermined faith in the political system, creating space for insurgent candidates like Donald Trump — and Bernie Sanders.'

The potency of his message

It has always been true of presidential campaigns that in order to win, you don't just need a *good* message, you need *the right* message. You need to be talking about the very things that voters want to hear. The classic example of this was in the general election in 1992. President George H. W. Bush had a great message about foreign policy — how the Cold War was over, the Soviet Union had crumbled, Kuwait had been freed from the Iraqis and so on. But most Americans were not listening. They wanted to hear about economic policy, and along came Bill Clinton talking about the economy.

From years of listening to conservative talk radio, Trump knew the message and the policies that would get the grassroots of the Republican Party fired up — illegal immigration, terrorism, trade and entitlement programmes. Trump knew that first and foremost conservative, working-class voters were deeply concerned about illegal immigration. After the defeat of their candidate Mitt Romney in 2012, Republican leaders were convinced that their only way back to the White House was to enhance their appeal to racial minority voters. Immigrants were now to be seen as new voters to court. But blue-collar Republicans saw them as people filling their schools and taking their jobs. They saw illegal immigration as a threat to America — to its economy, its culture and its security.

Therefore, by promising to deport millions of illegal immigrants and build a wall across America's border with Mexico, Trump both established his conservative credentials and sharply differentiated himself from all the other Republican candidates. Of course, Trump knew that his racially charged harangues would be condemned by the mainstream media and by the Republican leadership. But Trump reckoned — correctly as it turned out — that this would merely enhance his reputation among his own supporters. The data in Table 3.5 show that of the 50% of Alabama Republicans who stated that illegal immigrants working in United States should be deported to their home country, 58% voted for Trump. The idea may have appalled many, but it was clearly very appealing to others.

Table 3.5 Alabama Republican Primary exit poll data
Q: Illegal immigrants working in the US should be...

Candidate	Offered legal status (45%)	Deported to home country (50%)
Jeb Bush	0%	1%
Ben Carson	13	8
Ted Cruz	18	21
John Kasich	9	2
Marco Rubio	29	9
Donald Trump	29	58

Linked with fears over illegal immigration were fears of terrorism, perpetrated by those who had legally entered the USA or who were even now American citizens, but whose political sympathies lay with radical terrorist groups with links to the Middle East. So after the deadly attacks committed by jihadists in Paris in November 2015, Trump repeated his discredited statement that thousands of American Muslims in New Jersey had celebrated the 9/11 attacks in New York by dancing in the streets — a baseless lie without one shred of evidence. He then went further and called for a blanket ban on all Muslims entering the United States (see Box 3.1), even going so far as to suggest that all Muslims in America might need registering and monitoring. All this was repeated following the gun massacres in San Bernardino, California, in December 2015 and in Orlando, Florida, in June 2016. In the Alabama Republican Primary, 78% of voters supported Trump's ban on Muslims entering the United States, and they overwhelmingly voted for Trump (see Table 3.6).

Table 3.6 Alabama Republican Primary exit poll data

Q: Do you support or oppose a temporary ban on Muslims entering the United States?

Candidate	Support (78%)	Oppose (19%)
Jeb Bush	1%	0%
Ben Carson	8	14
Ted Cruz	21	14
John Kasich	2	17
Marco Rubio	14	36
Donald Trump	52	17

Table 3.7 Republican leadership v. Trump on selected issues

Policy	Republican leadership's position	Trump's position
Immigration	• saw immigrants as potential new voters	• saw immigrants as posing an economic, cultural and security threat
Terrorism	• advocated covert measures such as intelligence gathering; measures that were generally discreet but effective	• advocated overt measures such as deportation, overt surveillance of certain racial and religious groups
Trade	• advocated international trade deals; pro-free trade	• claimed such deals were a sell-out by weak leaders
Tax and entitlements	• advocated tax cuts for the better off but cuts in entitlement programmes	• supported current levels of spending on entitlement programmes

In the areas of both immigration and terrorism, Trump was being iconoclastic, deviating wildly from the conventional wisdom of the Republican hierarchy. It was the same on trade. For decades, the Republican leadership had gone along with — even promoted — trade deals with the likes of China and Mexico. But blue-collar Republicans saw them as a sell-out, sending jobs away from their towns and cities to workers in foreign countries. Then along came Donald Trump and publicly bashed the international trade deals so dear to his party's business allies and free trade gurus. According to Trump, such trade deals were a sell-out by weak, clueless leaders. The solution, he said, was simple: 'Make America Great Again!' and put 'America First'. He would abandon free trade agreements and 'bring back our jobs' from overseas. If American companies moved jobs abroad, then under President Trump there would be 'consequences — and they will be very serious consequences'.

Finally, there was the area of tax and entitlements. Entitlements are benefits provided by the government to which recipients have a legal right based on age, occupation or income — such as Social Security, Medicare and Medicaid. Here again, the Republican leadership were out of touch with their blue-collar supporters. Following the economic crisis of 2008, their policy was to bail out the banks and offer tax cuts to the better off, but cut entitlement programmes. Furthermore, Republican leaders in Congress took the rejection of Obamacare as a rejection of social welfare programmes as a whole, despite polling evidence showing that blue-collar workers still supported spending that they believed they deserved, like Social Security and Medicare.

Conclusions

So Trump won the nomination because of his status as a pop culture icon, the disaffectedness of a sizable chunk of the Republican electorate, and a message which resonated with them. But he also needed a medium by which to convey that message. And that medium was television. To the struggling television companies, a candidate like Trump was a godsend. According to Ann Curry, a former anchor of NBC's *Today* show, 'Trump stepped on to the presidential campaign stage precisely at a moment when the media was struggling against deep insecurities about its financial future. The truth is,' said Curry, 'the media needed Trump.' And because Trump was Trump, the media allowed him to get away with things that regular politicians would not have got away with. Television executives knew Trump was good for their ratings.

There were other contributors to Trump's victory. The Republican Party leadership hugely underestimated Trump until it was too late. His fellow Republican candidates were far too slow to challenge him on his lies and insinuations. The fact that there were so many candidates meant that Trump could win races with a small percentage of the vote. And the 2016 Republican field — though one of the largest on record — was also one of the weakest. Had there been a Bill Clinton or a Ronald Reagan among them, Trump would probably have withered before the snow had melted in New Hampshire. Even the Republicans' own candidate selection process, with its lack of super delegates and its winner-takes-all or winner-takes-most primaries, contributed to Trump's victory parade. Although Trump continually referred to the selection process as 'totally rigged', Table 3.2 shows us that Trump won 58% of the delegates on the basis of 45% of the votes. There is every reason to believe that, had the Republicans used a selection process identical to that of the Democrats, Trump would not have been selected as their presidential candidate. But despite all the self-congratulations, Trump recorded the lowest share of the popular vote of any winning candidate in a contested Republican contest in over 40 years (see Table 3.8). What is more, no candidate had won less than 59% of the primary vote and won in November.

Table 3.8 Percentage of popular vote by winning Republican in contested presidential primaries, 1976–2016

Candidate	Year	% of popular vote
George H. W. Bush	1992	72.8
George H. W. Bush	**1988**	**67.9**
George W. Bush	**2000**	**62.0**
Ronald Reagan	**1980**	**59.8**
Bob Dole	1996	58.8
Gerald Ford	1976	53.3
Mitt Romney	2012	52.1
John McCain	2008	47.3
Donald Trump	**2016**	**45.0**

Bold: won in November election

What was more, Trump had failed to bring the party together at the end of the nomination process, despite his claims to the contrary. Trump's claims that 'I'm a unifier, and we're going to be a united party' were rather contradicted by the way in which his opponents had talked about him, and he was still talking about them. Trump claimed that he could and would change, but as spring turned into summer, the evidence of any change in tone or temper was hard to see. Trump had defied conventional wisdom and won the nomination, but could he win the presidency? As the party convention approached, the omens for Trump and his fellow Republicans were not good.

A final observation. In the RealClearPolitics poll average on 1 September 2015, Clinton was on 48.6% and Trump on 42%. Exactly a year later, after all the primaries and caucuses, the televised candidate debates, two party conventions and $992 million of candidate spending, Clinton was on 48.3% and Trump on 42.3%. The polls had shifted 0.3%. One was left asking whether it had really all been worth it.

Questions

1 What is the track record of the Republican Iowa caucuses in identifying the eventual nominee?
2 What happened on Super Tuesday in the Republican race and why was it significant?
3 Explain the term 'brokered convention'.
4 What happened in the Republican race between mid-March and mid-April?
5 Why was there a discrepancy between Trump's final popular vote percentage and his share of the delegates?
6 How do the data in Tables 3.3 and 3.4, and in Figure 3.1, help explain Trump's victory in the Republican primaries?
7 Why did many Republicans feel betrayed by their own party leadership?
8 What policies did Trump advocate to appeal to blue-collar Republicans?
9 What potential future problems for Trump did the primaries foreshadow?

Chapter 4

The conventions: hope trumps fear

What you need to know

- National party conventions meet for about four days during the summer of each presidential election year.
- By tradition, the 'challenging party' — the Republicans in 2016 — holds its convention first.
- The conventions are attended by delegates who are mostly chosen during the primaries and caucuses.
- The conventions are said to have three main functions: choosing the party's presidential candidate; choosing the party's vice-presidential candidate; deciding on the party platform, i.e. the manifesto.
- But nowadays all three functions are done before the conventions meet.
- The significance of modern-day conventions is therefore questionable.

Why conventions still matter

Half a century ago, national party conventions actually chose the presidential candidates. But that all changed from the 1970s onwards. And for all the media chatter about the Republicans possibly having a 'brokered convention' this time around, as we all know that came to nothing. So today it's easy to write off the conventions as no more than balloon-infested infomercials with silly people in silly hats pretending to do and say something important.

But there is another side to this. True, the modern-day conventions do not make any significant decisions, but they still play an important role at a critical juncture in the presidential campaign, for three reasons. First, they are the first time many Americans tune into the campaign. That's especially true of independent voters, most of whom do not participate in the primaries. Second, they are almost the only opportunity the candidates get to introduce themselves — directly and unfiltered by the media — to potential voters. They will never again, for example, have an hour's free, uninterrupted airtime to address the voters as they do in their convention acceptance speeches. And third, it has proved very difficult to win the presidency in modern times without emerging from the conventions ahead in the polls. The only two exceptions are Ronald Reagan in 1980, who was merely tied with Jimmy Carter but went on to win comfortably, and George W. Bush, who trailed Al Gore in 2000 — but although he won the election, he did of course lose the popular vote.

When it came to the conventions of 2016, one could summarise them as two stories — one of fear, the other of hope.

Fear: the Republicans in Cleveland

Pre-convention manoeuvring

As the Republicans gathered in Cleveland, Ohio, for their national convention in mid-July, the party had still not united around its presumptive nominee Donald Trump. There were glaring problems concerning a lack of organisation, money and policy detail for anyone — whose surname was not Trump — to see. Even two days out from the convention, there was no advertised programme, just a vague list of speakers — many who shared the same surname, beginning with 'T'. If running a convention was proving such a challenge to Team Trump, one wondered how they would cope when it came to running a nationwide campaign, or a country.

Box 4.1	Themes and main speakers, Republican national convention

Monday 18 July: 'Make America Safe Again'

- Rick Perry, former governor of Texas
- Rudy Giuliani, former mayor of New York
- Melania Trump, wife of Donald Trump

Tuesday 19 July: 'Make America Work Again'

- Senator Mitch McConnell, Senate Majority Leader
- Congressman Paul Ryan, House Speaker
- Governor Chris Christie of New Jersey
- Tiffany Trump, daughter of Donald Trump
- Donald Trump, Jr, son of Donald Trump
- Ben Carson, retired neurosurgeon

Wednesday 20 July: 'Make America First Again'

- Governor Scott Walker of Wisconsin
- Senator Marco Rubio of Florida
- Senator Ted Cruz of Texas
- Eric Trump, son of Donald Trump
- Newt Gingrich, former House Speaker
- Governor Mike Pence of Indiana — acceptance speech

Thursday 21 July: 'Make America One Again'

- Ivanka Trump, daughter of Donald Trump
- Donald Trump — acceptance speech

Before the convention opened, Trump had announced his choice of Mike Pence, the governor of Indiana, former US congressman and Tea Party movement supporter, as his vice-presidential running mate. The other two 'finalists' had been Governor Chris Christie of New Jersey and the former House Speaker, Newt Gingrich. Trump doubtless thought Christie and Gingrich too Trump-like in their publicity-seeking demeanour to want to have them on the ticket with him. Trump is not one to encourage competition for the limelight. In this sense, Mike Pence was ideal — quiet and unassuming in character, but with views well to the right of most general election voters. Certainly Trump was not trying to add to his Electoral College Vote tally. Indiana, with its 11 electoral votes, had voted Republican in every election since 1968.

The Platform Committee also met in the week before the convention to finalise the party platform. Among what would be regarded as its more controversial items were calls to:

- overturn the Supreme Court decisions on same-sex marriage
- ban all types of abortion, without exception
- oppose any limits on the magazine capacity of guns
- build a wall along the USA–Mexico border

These and other policy proposals reflected the stance taken by Donald Trump during the primaries and therefore showed another way in which the New York tycoon had imposed himself on the party.

Also before the convention, the attempt by Trump's most ardent opponents within the party to allow the delegates to vote with 'their conscience' rather than for the candidate to whom they were committed from the primaries was easily defeated (87–12) in the party's rules committee.

Four days of fear

But as dawn broke over Ohio that Monday morning, there was still one faint hope: that Donald Trump would pivot from his hateful rage of the primaries and appear — to quote the first President Bush — in his 'kinder, gentler' self. Maybe after all Trump would appear as a graceful, statesmanlike figure, speaking with courage but also with magnanimity, offering carefully crafted and costed policies to raise and inspire the nation. And if that happened, then maybe party unity would suddenly break out and the Republicans could enter the campaign against Hillary Clinton in a spirit of togetherness and optimism — both for themselves and for the country. It would prove to be a false hope.

Each day was assigned a theme (see Box 4.1) which played on the overall 'Make America Great Again' theme. One might therefore have expected the focus to be on different policy themes each day. But that was hardly discernible. Monday — 'Make America Safe Again' — featured a rules fight and a part-plagiarised speech. The rules fight occurred when the anti-Trump delegates tried to force a roll call vote on the party's convention rules that had been agreed in committee the previous week. This was the last chance saloon for #NeverTrump and again it failed, though not without some rancorous scenes on the convention floor.

But the real brouhaha of Monday concerned the speech delivered by Melania Trump, the wife of the presumptive nominee. The initial reaction to her speech was positive. She had, as it were, cleared the low bar of expectations. But some hours later, the twitter-sphere and the internet lit up with allegations that Mrs

Box 4.2 Michelle Obama (2008) and Melania Trump (2016) speeches compared

Michelle Obama Democratic National Convention (2008)	Melania Trump Republican National Convention (2016)
And Barack and I were raised with so many of the *same* values: that you work hard for what you want in life; that your word is your bond and you do what you say *you're going to do;* that you treat people with *dignity and* respect, *even if you don't know them, and even if you don't agree with them. And Barack and I set out to build lives guided by these values, and pass them on to the next generation.* Because we want our children — *and all children* in this nation — to know that the only limit to *the height of* your achievements is the *reach* of your dreams and your willingness to work for them.	*From a young age my parents impressed on me* the values that you work hard for what you want in life; that your word is your bond and you do what you say *and keep your promise.* That you treat people with respect. *They taught and showed me values and morals in their daily life.* *That is a lesson that I continue to pass along to our son, and need to pass those lessons on to the many generations to follow* because we want our children in this nation — to know that the only limit to your achievements is the strength of your dreams and your willingness to work for them.

Source: www.washingtonpost.com

Trump had plagiarised parts of a speech delivered by Michelle Obama to the Democratic convention in 2008 (see Box 4.2). When in 2008 Barack Obama was accused of plagiarising part of a speech by the then governor of Massachusetts, Deval Patrick, Obama apologised, saying it would have been better to have attributed those words to Patrick. But the reaction of Team Trump? Simply deny it — until some days later when a young speech writer was forced to offer a public apology. The moral of the story? The Trumps don't admit mistakes.

Tuesday — 'Make America Work Again' — featured two somewhat bizarre speeches from two of Trump's former primary opponents. Chris Christie indulged in a mock trial of Hillary Clinton inviting the delegates to respond with either 'guilty' or 'not guilty' to each apparent charge that he read out. Needless to say, only cries of 'guilty' were to be heard, along with what was to become the delegates' favourite chant of the week each time the name of the presumptive Democratic nominee was mentioned, 'Lock her up! Lock her up!' I don't think any convention before had featured delegates repeatedly calling for the opposing party's nominee to be imprisoned. That said, worse was to come when Al Baldasaro, Trump's adviser on veterans' affairs, used a television interview to call for Hillary Clinton to be 'put in a firing line and shot for treason'. The Secret Service said they were investigating. In his speech, Ben Carson managed to somehow link the name of Mrs Clinton with that of the devil. Welcome to the Salem Witch Trials, reborn in 2016. Perhaps things could only get better.

Table 4.1 Final delegate votes in roll call of the states, Republican convention

Candidate	Delegate votes
Donald Trump	1,725
Ted Cruz	484
John Kasich	125
Marco Rubio	123
Ben Carson	7
Jeb Bush	3
Rand Paul	2
Abstained	3

But Wednesday brought us Ted Cruz. The junior senator from Texas had been Trump's nearest rival during the primaries before exiting the race in early May. In the early months, Cruz had been careful not to join in the bashing of Trump, always referring to him as 'Donald' in the early debates. But things turned nasty as Cruz threatened Trump's lead and from then on Cruz was always 'Lyin' Ted' in Trump's speeches and Trump made personal attacks on Cruz's wife and father. At the eleventh hour, Cruz agreed to address the convention, spoke for 20 minutes, but failed to endorse the nominee, closing with his call to 'vote your conscience' rather than 'vote for Trump'. Trump delegates were infuriated and booed Cruz off the stage. Not good for party unity, though one has the sneaking suspicion that Cruz's refusal to endorse Trump had more to do with Cruz's ambitions for 2020 than with taking any moral stand. Cruz's antics also completely overshadowed an entirely forgettable acceptance speech by Mike Pence, who was in danger of becoming the campaign ghost — making a fleeting appearance before disappearing, never to be seen again. Wednesday also brought the traditional roll call of states to formally nominate Donald Trump, with Trump finally winning the votes of 1,725 — or just under 70% — of the 2,472 delegates (see Table 4.1).

And then, finally, there was Donald Trump's acceptance speech. Ronald Reagan, making a farewell appearance at the Republicans' 1992 convention, said this: 'Whatever else history may say about me when I'm gone, I hope it will record that I appealed to your best hopes, not your worst fears.' He was right. He always did. For Reagan, it was 'Morning Again In America'. Trump is the polar opposite. He always, incessantly, interminably, talks (or shouts) about America's very worst fears. This is '*Mourning* Again In America' — a litany of violence, killings, shootings, murders, brutality, terrorism, war, destruction, hatred, chaos, danger and disaster (see Box 4.3).

It was apocalyptic in its content, and Nuremberg-like in its strident and loud theatrics. 'Nobody knows the system better than me,' boasted Trump, 'which is why *I alone* can fix it.' 'I alone'? This was either a candidate who was ignorant of even the basic principles of American government — a government of 'shared powers' — or a candidate who saw himself as *Il Duce*. I wasn't sure which of the

> ### Box 4.3 Selected words and phrases of Trump's acceptance speech
>
> crisis · attacks · terrorism · danger · **violence** in our streets · chaos in our communities · **violence** · crime · **violence** · crime · *homicides* · *killings* · *shootings* · *killed* · *killed* · criminals · *killed* · *killer* · poverty · poverty · debt · falling apart · poverty · humiliation · at gunpoint · one international humiliation after another · forced to their knees · brought down in flames · far less safe · in ruins · helpless to die at the hands of savage *killers* · chaos · wars · crisis · war · poverty and **violence** at home · war and destruction abroad · rigged political and economic system · horrible and unfair trade deals · communities crushed · brutally *executed* · threats and **violence** · *shot* or *killed* · *gunned down* · *killed* · very badly injured · brutal Islamic terrorism · *viciously mowed down* · lives ruined · families ripped apart · a nation in mourning · damage and devastation · *savagely murdered* · terrorist · terrorist · **violence** and oppression · hateful foreign ideology · **violence**, hatred or oppression · *killed* by illegal immigrants · **violence** spilling across our borders · *brutally murdered* · suffered so horribly · wounded American families · gangs and **violence** · mass lawlessness · worst economic deals · colossal mistakes and disasters · total disaster

two I wanted to opt for. Indeed, I have to admit that never before have I felt so uncomfortable watching, or now writing about, an American political event. This was 'Make America *Hate* Again'. Its incessant dog whistle of 'law and order' with its insinuation — no, he actually said it — that America is now a country in which law-abiding, native-born Americans are to be 'killed by illegal immigrants' was, quite simply, racist. This was 'Make America *White* Again'. The rasping tone was deeply troubling. Ah, maybe that was what Trump had in mind — 'Make America *Grate* Again'!

Hope: the Democrats in Philadelphia

Pre-convention manoeuvring

It's only 431 miles from Cleveland to Philadelphia. American Airlines fly it in just 85 minutes. In UK terms, it's London to Glasgow. In American terms it's no distance at all. But for all their geographic proximity, when it came to tone and temper these two conventions might as well have been on different planets. This was not so much just *A Tale of Two Cities*, more a 'tale of two countries'. To continue the Dickensian theme, at Cleveland it had been 'the worst of times'; now at Philadelphia it was for the most part 'the best of times' — unless, maybe, you were a die-hard Bernie Sanders delegate. To switch from Dickens to Churchill, if Trump had been determined to paint a picture of America in 'the abyss of a new dark age', then Clinton was heading for 'the broad, sunlit uplands' and America's 'finest hour'.

Less than 48 hours after the close of the Republican proceedings in Cleveland, Hillary Clinton had announced her choice of Senator Tim Kaine of Virginia as her vice-presidential running mate. If the first rule of selecting one's running mate is 'do no harm', then Hillary Clinton hit a home run. In a year of the weird — Trump, Cruz, Perry, Sanders, Carson — Kaine brought a welcome dose of normality. In a year of flamboyance, Kaine brought modesty. In a year of candidates who seemed to be boastful moral vacuums surrounded by gilded luxuries, Kaine came as the candidate who attends the same church in which he and his wife were married, has served as a Christian missionary in Honduras, and has lived in the same house for the last 24 years. True, the Sanders supporters were disappointed, hoping for a firebrand like Senator Elizabeth Warren. But Clinton was looking past the campaign, in the same way that George W. Bush was when he chose Dick Cheney 16 years earlier. She was looking to governing, not campaigning. The fact that Kaine had served both as governor and as senator in a swing state was a happy coincidence. Virginia's 13 electoral votes now looked to be more solidly in the Democratic column.

Four days of hope

At Cleveland, Trump had struggled to get the party's House members, senators and state governors to speak for him, and even some of those who did were not exactly fulsome in their support. It was all change in Philadelphia, where 37 Democratic House members, 16 senators and 7 state governors took to the platform to enthusiastically endorse Hillary Clinton as 'the next president of the United States of America'.

Box 4.4 **Themes and main speakers, Democratic national convention**

Monday 25 July: 'United Together'

- First Lady Michelle Obama
- Senator Elizabeth Warren of Massachusetts
- Senator Bernie Sanders of Vermont

Tuesday 26 July: 'A Lifetime of Fighting for Children and Families'

- Jimmy Carter (via video)
- Bill Clinton

Wednesday 27 July: 'Working Together'

- Vice President Joe Biden
- Senator Tim Kaine of Virginia — acceptance speech
- President Barack Obama

Thursday 28 July: 'Stronger Together'

- Khizr Kahn, father of fallen Army Captain Humayun Khan
- Chelsea Clinton, daughter of Hillary Clinton
- Hillary Clinton — acceptance speech

The first day did not exactly run smoothly, and the day's theme 'United Together' appeared more fanciful that fact. The most ardent of Bernie Sanders' supporters booed every mention of Hillary Clinton's name, even during the opening benediction. Sanders himself was saying in every way he could that he was now fully on board the Hillary Clinton Express. It was just that having wound up his youthful supporters to such a pitch for the previous nine months and more, it was proving difficult to get them to accept Clinton as their nominee. Indeed, the first day could have careened out of control had it not been rescued by a barnstorming performance from First Lady Michelle Obama. No wonder Mrs Trump wanted to sound like her! The first lady made not-so-veiled references to the Republican nominee and united the convention by doing it with grace and humour (see Box 4.5).

Box 4.5 **Extracts from Michelle Obama's convention speech**

… How we insist [to our daughters] that hateful language they hear from public figures on TV does not represent the true spirit of this country. How we explain that when someone is cruel, or acts like a bully, you don't stoop to their level. No — our motto is, 'When they go low, we go high'.

And when I think about the kind of president that I want for our girls and all our children, I want someone with the proven strength to persevere. Someone who knows this job and takes it seriously. Someone who understands that the issues a president faces are not black and white and cannot be boiled down to 140 characters. Because when you have the nuclear codes at your fingertips and the military in your command, you can't make snap decisions. You can't have a thin skin or a tendency to lash out. You need to be steady, and measured, and well informed.

In his speech, Bernie Sanders did well to tread a fine line between speaking for his own supporters and loyally and whole-heartedly supporting the nominee. But unlike Ted Cruz's 'vote your conscience' line at the end of his speech in Cleveland, Bernie Sanders closed with this ringing endorsement of Hillary Clinton:

> I have known Hillary Clinton for 25 years. I remember her as a great first lady who broke precedent in terms of the role that a first lady was supposed to play as she helped lead the fight for universal health care. I served with her in the United States Senate and know her as a fierce advocate for the rights of children. Hillary Clinton will make an outstanding president and I am proud to stand with her here tonight.

There are four former living presidents still alive — two Republicans (George H. W. and George W. Bush) and two Democrats (Jimmy Carter and Bill Clinton). Neither of the Bushes was prepared to grace the Republican gathering in Cleveland, but Tuesday night in Philadelphia featured both Carter and Clinton. Via a live video link, Carter, now 91, described Trump as someone who 'violates the moral and ethical principles upon which our nation was founded' and pledged his support to Hillary Clinton. Bill Clinton, whose first national convention speech back in 1988 was panned for being overly long and boring, spoke eloquently of the more personal and hidden side of his spouse, as well as describing her as 'the best darned change-maker I've ever known'.

Tuesday evening also saw the roll call of the states as the delegations announced their votes — for Clinton or Sanders. In the final delegate count, Hillary Clinton won just under 60% of the votes to just under 40% for Bernie Sanders (see Table 4.2). Then, at the end of the roll call, Sanders took to the microphone to 'move that all votes cast by delegates be reflected in the official record, and I move that Hillary Clinton be selected as the nominee of the Democratic Party for president of the United States'. In 2008, Hillary Clinton had asked the convention to select Obama 'by acclamation'. Sanders did not go that far, but this was as good as party unity was going to get in 2016. By just before 7 p.m. on 26 July 2016, a major party had finally elected a woman as its presidential candidate — 32 years after first putting a woman in the number two slot, and 13 days after Britain had chosen its second woman prime minister. It certainly had taken long enough.

Table 4.2 Final delegate votes in roll call of the states, Democratic convention

Candidate	Delegate votes
Hillary Clinton	2,842
Bernie Sanders	1,865
Abstained	56

Wednesday evening featured Vice President Joe Biden on the subject of the Republican nominee:

> His cynicism is unbounded. His lack of empathy and compassion can be summed up in the phrase I suspect he's most proud of having made famous — 'You're fired!' Think about that! How can there be pleasure in saying 'you're fired'? He's telling us he cares about the middle classes. Give me a break! That's a bunch of malarkey!

The convention also heard Tim Kaine's acceptance speech, which he used firstly to introduce himself to the American people. He was not exactly a household name outside his home state of Virginia, having never before run for national office. The speech had two other motives: to make the case for Hillary Clinton and the case against Donald Trump. Kaine is a worthy speaker rather than an electrifying one, but he certainly passed this first test in the national spotlight with seeming effortless poise and command.

But the main speaker on this penultimate evening was President Obama. He, too, repeated the convention's theme of optimism and achievement. 'By so many measures, our country is stronger and more prosperous than it was when we started,' the president claimed. But this was not the usual speech of a two-term president coming to the end of his days, surveying his achievements and indulging in some self-congratulation. He wanted to fully endorse Hillary Clinton as his chosen successor. 'I can say with confidence,' Obama boomed with perhaps just a touch of hyperbole, 'that there has never been a man or a woman, not me, not Bill, nobody more qualified than Hillary Clinton to serve as president of the United States of America.' And he went after Trump.

Ronald Reagan called America 'a shining city on a hill'. Donald Trump calls it 'a divided crime scene' that only he can fix. It doesn't matter to him that illegal immigration and the crime rate are as low as they've been in decades, because he's not actually offering any real solutions to those issues. He's just offering slogans, and he's offering fear.

From time to time an ordinary citizen can play an outsize role in a national election campaign. It happened in the 2008 presidential election when Joe Wurzelbacher (alias 'Joe the Plumber') became an overnight star, having questioned then Senator Barack Obama about his small business policy while Obama was campaigning in Ohio. Joe the Plumber later appeared at campaign stops with Republican candidate John McCain and his name even featured in the third presidential debate. It happened in the 2010 UK general election when Gillian Duffy ambushed Prime Minister Gordon Brown, who was a few minutes later caught on a microphone in his car describing her as 'a bigoted woman'. It happened again in the 2016 election and this time featured Khizr and Ghazala Khan, the parents of fallen US Army captain Humayun Khan, who was killed in Iraq in 2004 and was buried at Arlington National Cemetery, just across the Potomac River from Washington DC. The Khans, who are of Pakistani heritage, had arrived in America in 1978.

The Khans took to the platform on the convention's final night and it was Khizr Khan who addressed the convention, charging Trump with 'smearing the character of Muslims' and 'disrespecting minorities' (see Box 4.6). But the most electrifying moments of Khizr Kahn's brief speech were his accusations that Trump might never have read the United States Constitution, and that Trump had 'sacrificed nothing and no one'.

Box 4.6 | **Extracts from Khizr Kahn's convention speech**

Donald Trump consistently smears the character of Muslims. He disrespects other minorities: women, judges, even his own party leadership. He vows to build walls, and ban us from this country. Donald Trump, you're asking Americans to trust you with their future.

Let me ask you, have you even read the United States Constitution? I will gladly lend you my copy. [He pulls copy from his pocket.] In this document, look for the words 'liberty' and 'equal protection of law'. Have you ever been to Arlington Cemetery? Go look at the graves of brave patriots who died defending the United States of America. You will see all faiths, genders and ethnicities. You have sacrificed nothing and no one.

The following day and with awful irony, Trump tweeted: 'Mr Khan, who has never met me, *has no right* [emphasis added] to stand in front of millions of people and claim that I have never read the Constitution.' Has no right? Even in his denial, Trump proved Mr Khan's underlying truth without even realising it. Appearing on ABC's *This Week with George Stephanopoulos* three days later, Trump not only defended himself against Khan's accusations but attacked both Khan and his wife (see Box 4.7). He even went so far as to equate the sacrifice the Khans had made with the 'sacrifices' he had made, such as 'working very hard' and 'creating thousands of jobs'. As former Obama strategist David Axelrod commented: 'I think people appreciate and even enjoy it when he kicks the high and mighty in the butt. But they recoil when he is unkind to ordinary people who are vulnerable, or when he is nasty to people who are thoroughly honourable.'

Box 4.7 **Donald Trump on ABC's *This Week* (extracts)**

George Stephanopoulos: ...Khizr Khan, the father of Humayun Khan, had some very tough questions for you. [Video clip from Khan's convention speech]

Donald Trump: I saw him, he was very emotional and probably looked like a nice guy to me. His wife, if you look at his wife — she was standing there — she had nothing to say, maybe she wasn't allowed to have anything to say. You tell me, but plenty of people have written that. She was extremely quiet, and looked like she had nothing to say. A lot of people have said that. And personally, I watched him, and I wish him the best of luck.

GS: He said that you have sacrificed nothing and no one.

DT: Well that's — who wrote that? Did Hillary's scriptwriter write it?

GS: But how would you answer that father? What sacrifices have you made for your country?

DT: I think I've made a lot of sacrifices. I work very, very hard. I've created thousands and thousands of jobs — tens of thousands of jobs. Built great structures. I've had tremendous success...

GS: Those are *sacrifices*?

DT: Sure, I think they're sacrifices.

There were a number of times during these four days when an observer might have mistaken this for a *Republican* convention — all that patriotic flag waving and talk of 'our beloved country' and 'enduring values', not to mention a strong defence and the American military as 'THE shining example of America at our very best'. Was this the same party that had hounded George W. Bush over Iraq in both 2004 and 2008?

The convention closed with Hillary Clinton's acceptance speech, having been introduced by her daughter Chelsea. One thing one needs to understand about Hillary Clinton is that she is an intensely personal individual. She doesn't let her guard down. She doesn't really do humour — and certainly not of the self-deprecatory kind. This has always been a Hillary problem and is one of the fundamental reasons why so few Americans think that she is a warm and likable person. What Clinton did succeed in doing was to paint a very contrasting picture of the country from the one on display in Cleveland the week before. The vocabulary was so different (see Box 4.8) as Clinton talked of a country not fearful, divided and in crisis, but hopeful, stronger and better together.

Box 4.8 Selected words and phrases of Clinton's acceptance speech

stronger · better · terrific · **together** · **stronger together** · dynamic and diverse · tolerant and generous · enduring values · freedom, equality, justice and opportunity · **together** · faith in each other · better and **stronger** · lift each other up · so happy · the sky's the limit · hardworking immigrants · **stronger** when we work with our allies · we have to heal the divides · keeping our country safe · none of us can do it alone · pulling **together** · **stronger together** · courage and confidence · our beloved country · greater than ever

The aftermath — convention 'bounce'

Convention bounce measures the change in the percentage support for the candidate in the final polls before the convention as compared with their support in the first polls after the convention. The average convention bounce for presidential candidates of the challenging party over the nine election cycles from 1980 through to 2012 was 6 percentage points. Trump's convention bounce was just over 1 percentage point, well below the average, and worse than all the last ten challenging candidates except for John Kerry (2004) and Mitt Romney (2012). And that included what was probably a rogue poll from CNN putting him on 48%. A week later, CNN put him back on 43%. Without that poll, Trump had no measurable bounce at all.

The average convention bounce for candidates of the president's party between 1980 and 2012 had been just over 5 percentage points. Clinton came in just below that at around 4.5 points. The picture was also distorted by the fact that Trump so dominated the news stories at the end of the Democratic convention through his criticism of the Khans that it was difficult to tell whether the polls were moving in approval of Clinton or disapproval of Trump — or both.

Table 4.3 CNN polls before/after Democratic convention compared

Category	Trump	Clinton
Favourability rating	Down 10	Up 3
Party united	Down 4	Up 9
Policies would take country in the right direction	Down 2	Up 5
Would feel proud of him/her as president	Down 9	Up 7
Is in touch with problems of ordinary Americans	Down 10	Up 4
Honest/trustworthy	Down 8	Up 4
Will unite the country	Down 9	Up 7

So who won the battle of the conventions? A CNN poll published a few days after the close of the Democratic convention showed some worrying signs for Donald Trump. The headline story was that from leading Clinton 48–45% in the pre-convention poll, Trump now trailed Clinton 52–43%. A 3-point lead had become a 9-point deficit in just one week. But dig deeper and the poll showed a host of worrying trends for Trump. His favourability rating had fallen by 10 points. His honest/trustworthy rating had fallen by 8 points. Fewer people thought the Republican Party was united. Fewer people thought Trump's policies would take the country in the right direction. Fewer said they would be proud to have him as their president. Fewer people thought he was in touch with the problems facing ordinary Americans. Fewer people thought he would unite the country. Clinton's numbers were up in all these categories (see Table 4.3). Maybe hope would trump fear after all.

Questions

1 What strengths did Mike Pence bring to the Republican ticket over either Christie or Gingrich?
2 What two final attempts did Trump's Republican opponents make to try to derail his nomination?
3 Why was Ted Cruz's convention speech so controversial?
4 Summarise Trump's acceptance speech in no more than 100 words.
5 What strengths did Tim Kaine bring to the Democratic ticket?
6 What part did Bernie Sanders and his supporters play at the Democratic convention?
7 How did Khizr Khan and his wife come to such prominence in the campaign both during and immediately after the Democratic convention?
8 In what ways did Hillary Clinton's acceptance speech differ from Trump's?
9 Who had the best convention — Trump or Clinton? (Give reasons for your answer.)

Chapter 5

The campaign

Trump slumps

As the general election campaigns kicked into top gear in August, Trump's poll numbers slumped — the effect of the conventions. His apocalyptic acceptance speech might have been well received in the convention hall in Cleveland, but it seemed unlikely to change the hearts and minds of many independent voters and did nothing to woo wavering Democrats. So in the first three weeks after the conventions, Trump's poll numbers dipped alarmingly, especially in crucial swing states that he really needed to win if he was going to have a realistic chance of winning this election. As a result, as Table 5.1 shows, his chance of winning states such as Arizona, Florida, Pennsylvania and Virginia — with a combined Electoral College vote of 73 — fell significantly. In Florida, in just three weeks, Trump went from a 75% chance of winning the state to just 41%. In Pennsylvania, he went from a 46% chance of winning the state to just 12%. And as Figure 5.1 shows (overleaf), in the national poll average Trump went from a 1-point lead on 27 July to an 8-point deficit just 13 days later (9 August). It was quite clear now who had won the conventions, and as a result who was winning the campaign, and it wasn't Trump.

Table 5.1 Chance of Trump winning in selected states: late July to mid-August

State	Date	Trump % chance of winning	Clinton % chance of winning	Change
Arizona	30 July	75	25	Trump −34
	14 August	41	58	
Florida	30 July	57	42	Trump −45
	15 August	12	87	
Pennsylvania	29 July	46	54	Trump −34
	17 August	12	87	
Virginia	29 July	44	56	Trump −35
	17 August	9	90	

Source: www.fivethirtyeight.com

Trump speaks

Trump's indiscipline on the campaign trail was already legion. Indeed, this was one of the reasons why his hardcore supporters liked him. Unlike professional politicians whose every word was sanitised and entirely politically correct, Trump was a loose cannon who would 'tell it the way it is'. But often to the frustration of his campaign team, Trump refused to tilt towards being more presidential now he was the Republicans' presidential candidate. He was still campaigning as he had always done.

On 2 August, he publicly refused to endorse Republican House Speaker Paul Ryan, who was facing a determined challenge in his congressional primary in Wisconsin. While campaigning in Virginia, Trump first praised Ryan's primary opponent Paul Nehlen for 'running a very good campaign', before telling the crowd:

> I like Paul, but these are horrible times for our country. We need very strong leadership. We need very, very strong leadership. And I'm just not quite there yet.

On the day he fell below 40% in the polling average for the first time since April, Trump was addressing a rally in Wilmington, North Carolina, ticking off the reasons to support him over Hillary Clinton, when he lingered longer on one reason. After accusing Clinton of wanting to remove Americans' gun rights, he continued that 'if she gets to pick her judges, nothing you can do folks'. Trump then paused and shrugged, before softly offering a postscript: 'Although the Second Amendment people, maybe there is, I don't know.' Critics took this as a thinly veiled invitation to gun owners to assassinate a future President Hillary Clinton. Trump, of course, blamed that interpretation on the evil and pro-Clinton media.

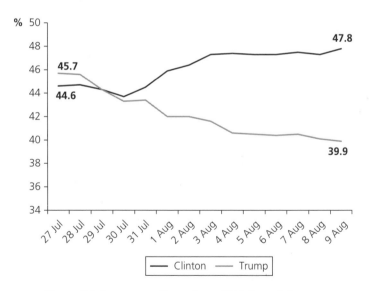

Figure 5.1 Average poll numbers: 27 July to 9 August

Source: www.realclearpolitics.com

For some weeks now, Trump had been suggesting that between them, Hillary Clinton and President Obama were in some way responsible for the emergence of so-called ISIS — the fundamentalist Islamist terror group. He began in June by suggesting that the president was an ISIS sympathiser. Then during an interview on CBS's *60 Minutes* in mid-July, he blurted out that 'Hillary Clinton invented ISIS with her stupid policies'. Two weeks later, he upgraded this is to the suggestion that Hillary Clinton 'should get an award from them as the founder of ISIS'. But at a rally in Fort Lauderdale, Florida, on 10 August — the day after the Second Amendment remark — Trump went full throttle. Speaking of ISIS, he now claimed:

> In many respects, you know, they honour President Obama. He's the founder of ISIS. He's the founder of ISIS. He's the founder. He founded ISIS.

The following day, Trump was offered numerous opportunities to back down from this patently foolish and ill-judged remark. Even the conservative radio host Hugh Hewitt, who had endorsed Trump, did pretty much everything he could to get Trump to retract the remark, but all in vain. 'I know what you meant,' Hewitt told Trump in a live interview. 'You meant that Obama created the vacuum when he lost the peace [in Iraq].' To which Trump replied, 'No, I meant he's the founder of ISIS.' At another rally later that day, Trump declared: 'I call President Obama and Hillary Clinton the founders of ISIS. They're the founders.'

Just in case there was still a scintilla of doubt, on 13 August, addressing a rally in Connecticut, Trump went for the Full Monty:

> ISIS has developed like wildfire under our incompetent President Obama, and I actually said to the press it's the opinion of myself and a lot of people that he was the founder of ISIS, that he's going to be presented over the next short period of time with the MVP award from ISIS — most valuable player.

Trump then descended the road marked self-pity and added:

> Can you imagine how badly I'll feel if I spent all that money, all of this energy, all of the time and LOST! I will never ever forgive the people of Connecticut. I will never forgive the people of Florida, and Pennsylvania, and Ohio.

Clinton frustrated...and collapsing

As the heat of August faded into a cooler September — climatologically, at least — Trump was beginning to claw his way back up in the polls, and as the date for the first of the three televised Clinton–Trump debates neared, Trump was now back to within a couple of points of his Democratic opponent. While Trump had imploded during and after the July conventions, Hillary Clinton had all but faded from view in the national media. But then she probably thought that if she just left Trump to push the self-destruct button, voters would come flocking to her cause.

That kind of strategy might have worked 20 years ago, but not in era of hyper-partisanship when the battle lines between Republicans and Democrats are so sharply drawn. And it wasn't going to work in 2016 — the election that pitted one historically unpopular, disliked and distrusted candidate against another historically unpopular, disliked and distrusted candidate. When likely voters were asked to express in their own words the main reason why they would vote for either Donald Trump or Hillary Clinton, the result was startling. As Table 5.2 shows, although qualifications, experience, issues, policies and personal qualities were mentioned by many voters, the most frequently given reason for their voting intention was their dislike of the other candidate. This seemed to give both candidates little opportunity to expand their voting base, leaving both to appeal merely to their own party base and 'preach to the choir'.

Table 5.2 Polling data on reasons for voting (%)

Q: In your own words, why are you most likely to vote for Clinton/Trump?

Factor	All voters	Clinton voters	Trump voters
Dislike opponent	28	28	28
Qualifications/experience	24	31	16
Issues/policies	17	11	23
Personal qualities	14	13	15
Party	9	12	6
Want change	4	1	9

Source: www.gallup.com

As Trump slowly clawed his way back up in the polls during the second half of August and September, Clinton was getting frustrated, and she wobbled — verbally and then physically. The verbal wobble — one should probably call it a gaffe — was to say at a rally in New York City on Friday, 9 September that 'you could put half of Trump's supporters into what I call the basket of deplorables'. In case you weren't entirely sure, Clinton then elaborated: 'The racist, sexist, homophobic, Islamaphobic — you name it — and Trump has lifted them up.' Soon Clinton would find herself apologising for these ill-chosen words, and finding them thrown back in her direction by Mr Trump.

After the verbal wobble came the physical wobble. Two days later, while attending an event in New York City to commemorate the 9/11 attacks, Clinton had to leave early, feeling unwell. But she was caught on camera collapsing as she was literally man-handled into her waiting security transport. For months, Trump had been trying to breathe life into an internet fable that Clinton was in declining health. These pictures merely gave further oxygen to the stories. And Clinton didn't help by the way she handled the story — first dismissing the whole thing as a minor hiccup, and only later admitting that she had been diagnosed with pneumonia. It was yet another example of Clinton's closed and secretive manner — one that makes her critics think she's deceptive and therefore untrustworthy.

Then, with just five days to go to the first debate, Clinton was taking part in a live video conference with the Laborers' International Union of North America — an organisation seeking to advance workers' rights in both the United States and Canada. Having reeled off all the ways she was worthy of their members' votes, Hillary asked rhetorically, 'So why aren't I 50 points ahead?' And it's a question that many Democrats must have asked since Trump was confirmed as

her Republican opponent. How, given all of the things that Donald Trump had said and done, was the race still quite close? How had an experienced politician like Clinton not buried her opponent by this stage in the campaign? Why wasn't she looking forward to a 1972- or 1984-style landslide? Aaron Blake writing in the *Washington Post* the following day suggested three reasons:

1 *Partisanship*. If you're a major party nominee these days, you've got to work pretty hard to get less than 40 or even 45% of the vote, because that's just how partisan the nation is at the moment. There are just so few genuine swing voters left, and while Trump certainly had his faults, he hadn't yet alienated that 40+% of partisan Republicans — and he probably never would.

2 *Enthusiasm*. Looking ahead to voter turnout on Election Day, enthusiasm for your candidacy is critical. And at this stage in the race, Trump supporters were more enthusiastic about Trump than Clinton supporters were about Clinton.

3 *Herself*. But the most significant reason why Hillary Clinton was not 50 points ahead — or any other double-digit amount — was the candidate herself. True, Trump's image numbers were bad, but so were hers — and that made for a close race. In a sharply polarised country, we had two sharply polarising candidates.

The first debate

With six weeks still to go to Election Day, Trump and Clinton met for their first televised encounter with a record 84 million Americans tuning in to watch the event on television. This beat the previous record of just over 80 million who watched the only debate between President Jimmy Carter and Governor Ronald Reagan in 1980. And that 84 million did not include the estimated 8 million who watched it via Facebook, or the estimated 2 million on YouTube. With two such controversial candidates, and Trump's unpredictability and proneness to shock, the hype was similar to that for a prize boxing contest or an evening of World Wrestling Entertainment.

But what Trump learnt — if he learnt anything at all — during this 90 minutes of mudslinging was that what had worked for him in the primaries didn't work for him now. Back in those Republican candidate debates, Trump had won by his hectoring one-liners, his abrasive manner, his interminable interruptions, his puerile pouting. In a debate with half-a-dozen other candidates (sometimes more), Trump could throw his political custard pies and then sit things out while the other candidates talked policies, before returning to the limelight to launch another volley of verbal vitriol. In the Theatre of the Absurd which was the Republican candidate debates, this strategy had worked. But in the forum that had been graced by former presidents — Ronald Reagan, Bill Clinton, Barack Obama and the like — he looked like and sounded like a miscreant fourth former trying to be clever in front of the serious scholar. His favourite word seemed to be 'wrong', which he interjected at numerous points throughout the evening (see Box 5.1), aiming it both at his Democratic opponent and at the hapless Lester Holt, who was trying to play the role of debate moderator and making something of a hash of it.

Extracts from transcript of first presidential debate, 26 September

CLINTON: You even suggested that you would try to negotiate down the national debt of the United States.

TRUMP: Wrong.

HOLT: Stop and Frisk was ruled unconstitutional in New York because it largely singled out black and Hispanic young men.

TRUMP: No, you're wrong.

CLINTON: Well, it's also fair to say, if we're going to talk about mayors, that under the current mayor [of New York City] crime has continued to drop, including murders. So there is —

TRUMP: You're wrong.

CLINTON: Well, I hope the fact checkers are turning up the volume and really working hard. Donald supported the invasion of Iraq.

TRUMP: Wrong.

CLINTON: That is absolutely proved over and over again.

TRUMP: Wrong.

CLINTON: He even said, you know, if there were nuclear war in East Asia, well, you know, that's fine, have a good time folks.

TRUMP: Wrong.

Clinton showed three strengths. First, she was exceedingly well prepared. Second, she knew exactly how to needle Trump, and did it time and again. Third, she kept her cool — and for most of the debate her smile. The lady in the red pant suit proved herself adept at throwing red meat in the direction of the Republican candidate, and he took the bait every time. So at one point, she speculated that Trump was refusing to release his tax returns simply because he had not paid any federal income tax. 'It would have been squandered,' blurted out Trump, noticeably failing to deny the allegation. And when Clinton went on to point out that Trump had probably not paid income tax for several years, Trump shot back, 'Which makes me smart!' That one would quickly appear in Clinton television ads. When she accused him of welcoming the housing market collapse in 2006 because he would profit financially from it, Trump retorted, 'That's called business.'

At one point, Trump tried to play Clinton's game and so decided to needle Mrs Clinton. In a somewhat rambling response to a question from Lester Holt, Trump responded:

> And I will tell you, you look at the inner cities, and I just left Detroit and I just left Philadelphia and I just — you know you've seen me, I've been all over the place. You decided to stay home, and that's OK. But I will tell you I've been all over, and I've met some of the greatest people I'll ever meet within these communities.

Trump was trying to draw attention to the well-publicised fact that in the days running up to the debate, while Hillary Clinton had played the teacher's pet, closeted in the library, doing her preparation, he had been enjoying himself, out and about with the lads. Mrs Clinton was ready for that. With a broad smile she responded:

> I think Donald just criticised me for preparing for this debate. And yes, I did. And you know what else I prepared for? I prepared to be president.

It was the revenge of the nerd. When Clinton at one point joked that 'I have a feeling that by the end of this evening, I'll be blamed for everything that ever happened', Trump retorted, 'Why not?' It sounded like the response of a petulant third grader and one couldn't help but think that the audience were actually laughing *at* him rather than *with* him. But in truth, this was no laughing matter. At first, Trump's poll numbers seemed to hold up, but within less than a week of the debate, his numbers started to tumble again, just as they had after the conventions. From a two-month high point of 45% in the RealClearPolitics poll average, Trump dropped 4 points in two weeks. In the week before the first debate, Trump had been just 1 point behind Clinton. By mid-October he was nearly 7 points adrift.

The second debate

The second debate was scheduled for Sunday, 9 October, but just 48 hours before the event the Trump campaign was rocked by a bombshell. This took the form of a videotape, recorded in 2005, in which Donald Trump bragged in the most vulgar terms about kissing, groping and trying to have sex with different women — even women he knew to be married. Trump boasted, 'When you're a star, they let you do it. You can do anything.' The public release of the tape was followed by hours of deafening silence — from the man who boasts of the motto, 'Never apologise'.

Late on the Friday evening, Trump issued a 90-second videotaped apology, recorded in his Trump Tower penthouse against a mock background of the New York City skyline. It was vintage Trump with its self-justification, acid attack and veiled threat. It began well enough.

> I've never said I'm a perfect person, nor pretended to be someone that I'm not. I've said and done things I regret, and the words released today on this more than a decade-old video are one of them. Anyone who knows me knows these words don't reflect who I am. I said it, I was wrong, and I apologise.

Trump then rambled about spending time with 'grieving mothers who've lost their children' and how he had been 'humbled by the faith they've placed in me'. With the apology out of the way from the now humbled candidate, Trump could return to what he does best — threaten and attack others, especially the Clintons.

> Let's be honest — we're living in the real world. This is nothing more than a distraction from the important issues we're facing today. We are losing our jobs, we're less safe than we were eight years ago, and Washington is totally broken. Hillary Clinton and her kind have run our country into the ground. I've said some foolish things, but there's a big difference between the words and

actions of other people. Bill Clinton has actually abused women, and Hillary has bullied, attacked, shamed and intimidated his victims. We will discuss this more in the coming days. See you at the debate on Sunday.

Trump seemed determined to be the man who always takes the low road, and then walks in the gutter. This, therefore, was the most extraordinary and excruciatingly embarrassing backdrop to the second debate. It was time for Hillary Clinton to take a leaf out of Michelle Obama's book that 'when they go low, we go high'.

It can't be said that Clinton managed that. At times she looked awkward and embarrassed. Trump put in a more even performance than he did in the first debate, but his contributions were littered with ill-judged verbal missiles that at different times put him at odds with not just his Democratic opponent, but the moderators, his own running mate — even himself. It was more Robert Mugabe than Ronald Reagan.

| Box 5.2 | Extracts from transcript of second presidential debate, 9 October |

RADDATZ: Mr Trump, Mr Trump — I want to get to audience questions and online questions.

TRUMP: So she's allowed to say that, but I'm not allowed to respond. [Sarcastically] Sounds fair!

TRUMP: I'll tell you what, I didn't think I'd say this and I'm going to say it and hate to say it: If I win, I'm going to instruct the attorney general to get a special prosecutor to look into your situation because there's never been so many lies, so much deception.

CLINTON: It's just awfully good that someone with the temperament of Donald Trump is not in charge of the law of our country.

TRUMP: Because you'd be in jail.

COOPER: We have a question from Ken about healthcare.

TRUMP: I'd like to know why aren't you bringing up the e-mails? It hasn't been finished.

COOPER: Ken has a question.

TRUMP: Nice. One on three. [Presumably he meant to say 'three on one', indicating that he thought the two moderators were ganging up with Clinton against him.]

RADDATZ: Mr Trump, let me repeat the question. If you were president, what would you do about Syria and the humanitarian crisis in Aleppo? I want to remind you what your running mate said. He said provocations by Russia need to be met with American strength and if Russia continues to be involved in air-strikes along with the Syrian government forces of Assad, the United States of America should be prepared to use military force to strike the military targets of the Assad regime.

TRUMP: Okay. He and I haven't spoken and I disagree.

RADDATZ: You disagree with your running mate.

This was a town hall-style debate in which a number of the questions were asked by the audience, made up of undecided voters. It was jointly moderated by Anderson Cooper of CNN and Martha Raddatz of ABC, who certainly did a much more commendable job than Lester Holt had managed in the first debate.

Inevitably the matter of the Trump tape was raised. 'Are you both modelling appropriate behaviour for today's youth?' asked one audience member. Trump seemed to argue that because his behaviour was not as reprehensible as ISIS 'chopping heads off', it was, well, just 'locker room talk'. But the most alarming Trumpism during this second debate came in Trump's assertion that if he were in charge of the law in America, Hillary Clinton would be 'in jail' (see Box 5.2). For months now, Trump had approvingly allowed the crowds at his rallies to chant 'Lock her up!' at every mention of his opponent's name. Back at the Republican convention when this routine started, Trump was rather more cautious. As the delegates chanted, 'Lock her up! Lock her up!' Mr Trump shook his head and counter-proposed, 'Let's defeat her in November'. Back then, Trump was still masquerading as a democrat. Now all pretence had gone. He even threatened her with a special prosecutor. In America, special prosecutors are appointed in order to remove political influence from the justice system. But what Trump was now proposing was a special prosecutor for the express purpose of punishing a political opponent. What's more, he'd already announced the verdict and the sentence.

The real loser of this debate, and of these three days in October, wasn't so much Donald Trump — although his poll numbers continued to slide — but the Republican Party. With just a few praiseworthy exceptions, the party leadership and its elected representatives in Congress continued to try to have it both ways — to condemn what Trump said, but still support him as their candidate.

The third debate

By the time of the final debate, 19 October, there was a sense from most Americans that they just wanted to get it over with. Maybe it was ironic that the venue for this debate was Las Vegas, Nevada — the city known for its tacky and tawdry landscape, including one of Trump's oversized hotels. Dana Milbank, writing for the *Washington Post*, also noted another architectural irony.

> In the middle of the city, a few blocks from the hulking Trump International Hotel, the famous Mirage Volcano has been delighting tourists for 27 years with its faux eruptions, spewing fire, smoke and water 100 feet into the air. A small sign at the volcano's base announces, 'Volcano show erupts Sunday through Thursday, 8 p.m. to 9 p.m'. But there were a series of additional eruptions in Las Vegas on Wednesday night…Donald Trump erupted at 6.30 p.m. local time. And 6.34, and 6.48, and 6.52, and 6.54. And then at 7.06, the crater blew off, leaving a gaping caldera where Trump's presidential campaign once stood.

At one point, the audience erupted into laughter when Trump claimed that 'Nobody has more respect for women than I do. Nobody.' They erupted in shock when, as Hilary Clinton was talking about her proposed Social Security Trust Fund, Trump lent into his microphone and called out, 'Such a nasty woman!' But the major eruption occurred when moderator Chris Wallace of Fox News asked Donald Trump whether or not he would accept the result of election, come what may. (For the full text of this exchange, see Box 5.3.) After a lengthy discourse on what he still saw as 'a rigged system', Trump — pressed further by Wallace — answered: 'I'll tell you at the time. I'll keep you in suspense. Okay?' Hillary Clinton called Trump's response 'horrifying' and the media — both traditional and social — erupted in condemnation of a major party candidate refusing to promise to accept the result of an election. It was another consequential kick in the teeth for all those Republican politicians who had spent the past four months defending Trump.

Box 5.3 **Extract from transcript of third presidential debate, 19 October**

WALLACE: Mr Trump, you've been warning at rallies recently that this election is rigged and that Hillary Clinton is in the process of trying to steal it from you. Your running mate Governor Pence pledged on Sunday that he and you, his words, will absolutely accept the result of this election. Today, your daughter Ivanka said the same thing. I want to ask you here on stage tonight, do you make the same commitment that you'll absolutely accept the result of this election?

TRUMP: I will look at it at the time. I'm not looking at anything now. I'll look at it at the time. What I've seen is so bad...It is so dishonest...I'll tell you one other thing. She shouldn't be allowed to run. She's guilty of a very, very serious crime. She should not be allowed to run, and just in that respect I say it's rigged.

WALLACE: But, sir, there is a tradition in this country, in fact one of the prides of this country is the peaceful transition of power no matter how hard fought a campaign is, that at the end of the campaign, that the loser concedes to the winner...Are you saying you're not prepared to commit to that principle?

TRUMP: What I'm saying is that I will tell you at the time. I'll keep you in suspense. Okay?

What happened in the polls?

In a rally in Sioux Center, Iowa (population 7,048) back in January, Trump had boasted that 'I have the most loyal people'. He then added: 'I could stand in the middle of Fifth Avenue and shoot somebody and I wouldn't lose any voters.' Perhaps the most extraordinary thing that we learnt during this campaign was that Trump was right — that whatever Donald Trump did or said, there was still a core of Americans who steadfastly stuck with him from one sordid surprise to another. And we would soon find out that this core was much bigger and more loyal than we thought.

If one looks at the poll average in the three-week period from 2 to 22 October, Clinton's support was relatively unchanged. Her numbers were never higher than

49% and never lower than 47.5%. Trump did fall — losing about 3 percentage points during this period (see Figure 5.2). Thus a 2.5-point deficit for Trump turned into a 6-point deficit during the period of the debates. But the graph also shows that the Trump videotape — made public on 7 October — did relatively little damage to Trump's support.

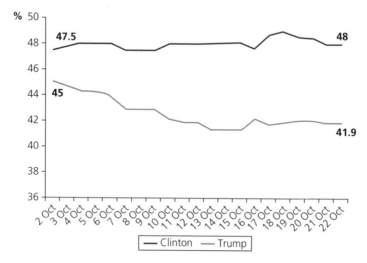

Figure 5.2 Average poll numbers: 2–22 October

Source: www.realclearpolitics.com

The October surprise

Steven Spielberg's 1978 horror thriller film *Jaws 2* — a film about shark attacks at a fictional seaside resort — spawned one of the great cinematic taglines of all-time: 'Just when you thought it was safe to go back in the water'. It could so easily have been adopted as a tagline for the 2016 presidential election. For just when you thought this election had nothing left to offer in the way of shocks and surprises, along came FBI Director James Comey with the October surprise to trump all October surprises.

| Box 5.4 | What is an October surprise? |

An October surprise is a development that occurs late in the presidential campaign — therefore usually in October — to the disadvantage of one candidate or campaign, the lateness of this development leaving the disadvantaged campaign/candidate with no adequate time to respond to it or recover from it before Election Day. The term was first used during the 1980 presidential election by Vice President Bush to suggest that President Carter might pull off a last-minute deal regarding the 52 American hostages held in Iran. Subsequent October surprises included the indictment of former Secretary of Defense Caspar Weinberger (30 October 1992), and press disclosure that George W. Bush had been involved in a drink-driving incident in 1976 (2 November 2000).

On 28 October, just 11 days before Election Day, FBI Director Comey sent a letter to certain members of Congress stating that he was reopening his investigation into Hillary Clinton's State Department e-mails — an investigation which he had announced was closed in early July — because of possible new information that 'appeared to be pertinent' to the Clinton e-mail investigation. This new material had apparently come to light during an unrelated investigation into former Democrat congressman Anthony Weiner, whose now estranged wife, Huma Abedin, was a top Clinton aide and vice chair of Clinton's presidential campaign committee. Comey's letter was big on seismic effect but remarkably thin on specificity. The news was greeted with glee by the Trump team and with gloom by Hillary Clinton, who demanded that Comey, in effect, put up or shut up. He should either put all the facts on the table, or exonerate her. Even President Obama did not sound too impressed with his FBI chief. 'We don't operate on innuendo,' said Obama in clear rebuke to Comey. 'We operate based on concrete decisions.'

So just as Clinton looked poised to expand her electoral map into Trump Country, her poll numbers — especially in some battleground states — started to dip and instead she found herself having to shore up her own territory with visits to Michigan, North Carolina and Pennsylvania.

And then just nine days after the first letter, there was a second Comey letter to Congress stating that nothing significant had been found after all and 'therefore we have not changed our conclusions that we expressed in July with respect to Secretary Clinton'. The whole episode reeked of ineptitude and bungling. It did allow Donald Trump another round of allegations about a 'rigged system', but the Comey letter probably did little to significantly erode Clinton's support. It was rather like the Trump video tape in that it didn't tell us anything about the candidate we didn't know before. We knew Trump was a moral vacuum. We knew the Clintons and scandal are close bedfellows. It had been a campaign of hate based on a parity of sleaze in which nothing much seemed to have changed, because there were no longer many voters whose minds were open to the idea of persuasion by the other side.

In the last nine weeks before Election Day, the RealClearPolitics website had published 95 Clinton–Trump polls: 6 showed the race tied, just 10 showed Trump ahead, and 79 showed Clinton leading — by a margin of anything between 1 and 14 points. So with Clinton ahead in the national polls as well as in most of the battleground states, we all knew exactly what would happen on Election Day. But then, just when you thought it was safe to declare Hillary Clinton the winner, the final excruciating twist in this election was about to unfold.

Questions

1 Explain why Trump's poll numbers slumped in the period between 27 July and 9 August.
2 How did Trump's indiscipline on the campaign trail show itself during August?
3 Explain the significance of the data in Table 5.2.
4 What problems did Clinton face in September?
5 Why wasn't she '50 points ahead' of Trump at this stage?
6 What strengths and weaknesses did Clinton and Trump show in the first debate?
7 What do the extracts from the second debate in Box 5.2 show about Trump?
8 What verbal bombshell did Trump drop during the third debate?
9 Analyse the data in Figure 5.2.
10 What is meant by an 'October surprise'? What was the October surprise of 2016?

Chapter 6

The result: an overview

Writing after the 2012 election, Dan Balz (*Collision 2012: Obama v. Romney and the Future of Elections in America*) had this to say about the brief intervention of Donald Trump in the Republicans' presidential nomination process.

> [By May 2011] Trump's phantom candidacy had peaked. A few weeks later, he announced to no one's surprise that he would not be a candidate. That Trump could become, even for a few weeks, a potentially serious choice in the minds of Republican voters highlighted a party whose leadership was being overrun by forces they could not control.

Just over five years later, the Trump forces had not only overrun the Republican Party, they had overrun the nation.

Pulling down the Blue Wall

By late morning on a sweltering day in August 2016, lines of Donald Trump supporters were queuing for more than four blocks along French and East 10th Street in Erie, Pennsylvania — a one-time booming industrial city on the shores of the lake that gives it its name — waiting to enter the Erie Insurance Arena. Many held umbrellas as they sought relief from the oppressive 80-degree heat. Some, like 60-year-old David Chundrlek and his two grandsons, were so determined to get in that they had arrived in the lakeside city — Pennsylvania's fourth largest — the previous night and had camped outside the arena's west entrance. 'I think Trump understands that things need to change in America,' Chundrlek said. 'He believes, like I do, it's about this country, and it needs to start moving forward instead of backward. He's not a perfect candidate, but I definitely like him and he stands for what I believe in.'

By early afternoon each of the 10,000 seats in the cavernous arena had been taken as Donald Trump walked on stage to a rapturous reception and the high-decibel rendering on the arena sound system of Lee Greenwood's 1984 number, 'God Bless the USA'. Trump did his usual stump ramble — one could not really call it a speech. But it was about jobs — American jobs — and how he was going to bring them back to America, from Mexico. One of the area's top employers, locomotive manufacturer GE Transportation, had laid off one-third of its employees in 2016. West 12th Street, once a bustling manufacturing corridor, was by now lined with towering edifices of empty factories and warehouses, and the city's population had fallen below 100,000 for the first time in nearly a century. Forty years ago, Erie won the All-American City Award. Now it was but a shadow of its former

self. Had the locals come up with a slogan to revitalise their now somewhat dreary city, it might have read something like 'Make Erie Great Again!'

But Erie, Pennsylvania — indeed, this whole swathe of Rust Belt states — was not exactly promising territory for Donald Trump. Pennsylvania, along with Michigan and Wisconsin, were part of what were called the Blue Wall of 18 states that had voted Democratic in all the six elections since 1992. Add to these three Iowa, which the Democrats had carried five times, and Ohio, which they had won four times, and together these five states held 70 Electoral College votes. In 2012, Mitt Romney had won 206 Electoral votes. So if Trump were to hold all of Romney's states and win these Rust Belt states, he had a path to the 270 votes he needed. And, as highly improbable as it seemed until the small hours of 9 November, that is precisely what Donald Trump did. Trump had run a campaign about building a wall — along the Mexican border. But his campaign was about pulling down a wall — that Blue Wall of states, behind which his Democratic opponent believed herself to be invulnerable.

Erie, in the furthest northwest corner of Pennsylvania, was the epitome of the kinds of place where Trump's message resonated. It has lost nearly 30% of its population in five decades. Around 75% of its population is white — higher than the national average; 19% of its population live below the poverty line. Unemployment had risen through 2016 from 5.1 to 7.1%. And when the votes were counted, Erie — which had given Obama a 17-point victory in 2012 — voted 49–47% for Donald Trump. It was the first time Erie had voted for a Republican presidential candidate since 1984.

And it was this story, repeated dozens of times across the Rust Belt, that gave Trump his totally unexpected victory. What was more, as we shall see, Trump was doing the same thing across much of rural America as well — especially in the nation's eastern half. Taking major hits in these kinds of communities, Hillary Clinton failed to make up for the losses in America's urban conurbations, failing even to match Obama's performance of either 2008 or 2012. Just days before the election, Clinton's campaign staff realised that some of her Blue Wall states were, after all, crumbling. They dispatched the candidate, and President Obama, to last-minute campaign stops in both Michigan and Pennsylvania. But it was too late. Clinton's failure to attract enough supporters in these and neighbouring Rust Belt states cost her the election, and shocked the world.

The result by the numbers

Whereas in 2012 only two states switched party control — Indiana and North Carolina both switching from Democrat to Republican — in 2016 six states switched, again all from Democrat to Republican. But these six states — Florida, Iowa, Michigan, Ohio, Pennsylvania and Wisconsin — had a combined Electoral College strength of 99 votes. Hence the profound implications of the Republican gains. Pennsylvania had not voted Republican in a presidential election since 1988, and Wisconsin not since the 49-state Reagan landslide of 1984. Ohio, meanwhile, made it 14 consecutive elections in which it had voted for the winning candidate — the bellwether state par excellence. But the state is clearly trending Republican. Trump won it by nearly 9 percentage points in an election in which he failed to win the popular vote.

But despite winning in the Electoral College by a comfortable margin of 77, Trump failed to win the popular vote, making this the second election in five in which the popular vote winner had lost in the Electoral College. This has now occurred four times in the nation's history, each time to the Republicans' advantage. One might expect to hear some harrumphing by Democrats against this archaic institution. But as the only way to reform or abolish it is by a constitutional amendment, don't expect any action. The reason why Clinton ended up with over 2 million more votes than Trump was that she was winning some large population states by very large margins — notably California by 2.7 million votes, and New York by 1.5 million. Hence, in a winner-take-all system, these 4.2 million votes were 'wasted votes' for Clinton. It was something of an irony that Trump's incessant claim that the electoral system was 'rigged' was, in this case, proved right. But it was rigged in his favour. It is also worthy of note that the Republicans have lost the popular vote in six of the last seven presidential elections — 2004 being the only exception between 1992 and 2016.

Table 6.1 Presidential election 2016: results by state, showing swing to the Republicans from 2012

State	Trump vote (%)	Clinton vote (%)	Swing to Republicans from 2012	Electoral College Trump (R)	Electoral College Clinton (D)
Alabama	63	35	+5	9	
Alaska	53	38	+3	3	
Arizona	49	45	−6	11	
Arkansas	60	34	+2	6	
California	33	62	−7		55
Colorado	44	47	+2		9
Connecticut	41	55	+3		7
Delaware	42	53	+8		3
Florida	**49**	**48**	**+2**	**29**	
Georgia	51	46	−3	16	
Hawaii	30	62	+11		3
Idaho	59	28	0	4	
Illinois	39	55	+1		20
Indiana	57	38	+9	11	
Iowa	**52**	**42**	**+16**	**6**	
Kansas	57	36	+1	6	
Kentucky	62	33	+6	8	
Louisiana	58	38	+2	8	

Table 6.1 Presidential election 2016: results by state, showing swing to the Republicans from 2012 (contd)

State	Trump vote (%)	Clinton vote (%)	Swing to Republicans from 2012	Electoral College Trump (R)	Clinton (D)
Maine	45	48	+12	1	3
Maryland	35	60	+1		10
Massachusetts	34	61	−4		11
Michigan	**48**	**47**	**+10**	**16**	
Minnesota	45	47	+6		10
Mississippi	58	40	+6	6	
Missouri	57	38	+9	10	
Montana	56	36	+6	3	
Nebraska	60	34	+4	4	
Nevada	45	48	+3		6
New Hampshire	47	48	+5		4
New Jersey	42	55	+4		14
New Mexico	40	48	+2		5
New York	37	59	+5		29
North Carolina	51	47	+2	15	
North Dakota	64	28	+17	3	
Ohio	**52**	**43**	**+11**	**18**	
Oklahoma	65	29	+2	7	
Oregon	41	52	+1		7
Pennsylvania	**49**	**48**	**+6**	**20**	
Rhode Island	40	55	+13		4
South Carolina	55	41	+3	9	
South Dakota	62	32	+12	3	
Tennessee	61	35	+6	11	
Texas	53	43	−6	36	
Utah	47	28	−29	6	
Vermont	33	61	+8		3
Virginia	45	50	−2		13
Washington	38	55	−3		8
West Virginia	69	26	+17	5	
Wisconsin	**48**	**47**	**+8**	**10**	
Wyoming	70	22	+7	3	
District of Columbia	4	93	−5		3
Totals	**46.0**	**48.1**	**+1.8**	**304**	**227**

Republican gains from 2012 in bold

US Government & Politics

Table 6.1 shows that in only nine states, plus the District of Columbia, did the Republicans *not* have a swing to them from 2012. The swing is the difference between the winning margins in the two elections. Thus in Ohio in 2012, the Democrats won by 2 percentage points. In 2016, the Republicans won Ohio by 9 points. Hence there was an 11-point swing to the Republicans. The states seeing the largest swings to the Republicans were North Dakota and West Virginia — both with a 17-point swing — and Iowa with a 16-point swing. At the other end of the scale, there was a 29-point swing against the Republicans in Utah, where Romney's 48-point win in 2012 was reduced to a 19-point win for Trump, but this was caused by the intervention of third-party candidate Evan McMullin who won 21% of the vote, rather than a revival in the Democrats' fortunes.

Of the 676 counties that voted for Obama in both 2008 and 2012, 209 (31%) voted for Trump in 2016. Erie County, Pennsylvania, was one that flipped. These Obama–Obama–Trump (OOT) counties were on average 81% white, whereas the remaining 467 Obama counties that voted for Clinton in 2016 were just 55% white. On top of that, the OOT counties had an average of 36% of voters who had no college education, compared with 28% in those counties that stayed with the Democrats. These are two voting blocs we shall be returning to later. Of the 207 counties that voted for Obama in either 2008 or 2012, 194 (94%) voted for Trump in 2016, with just 13 staying with Clinton. It was these 403 flipped counties that flipped the six states that gave Trump those extra 99 Electoral College votes.

Two other voting blocs we will need to investigate are white voters and older voters. Of the 250 counties with the most white voters, Trump won in 249 — Lake County, Minnesota being the one that got away. And of the 250 counties with the most voters aged 65 or older, Trump won in 241.

Maine, one of the two states that does not use a winner-take-all system for awarding its Electoral College votes — the other being Nebraska — split its electoral votes for the first time. Clinton won in the first congressional district (54–39%), Trump won in the second (51–41%) and Clinton won state-wide (48–45%). Therefore Clinton took 3 Electoral College votes and Trump 1. When the Electoral College voted on 19 December, Trump won 304 electoral votes to Clinton's 227, with four Clinton electors in Washington and one in Hawaii, as well as two Trump electors in Texas, failing to vote for their designated candidates.

The role of third parties

The role of third-party candidates Gary Johnson (Libertarian) and Jill Stein (Green) will doubtless be much analysed. Did they, like Green Party candidate Ralph Nader in 2000, affect the result of the election? Table 6.2 shows those five Trump states in which the combined Libertarian and Green Party vote was larger than the margin between Trump and Clinton.

Throughout the campaign, Johnson and Stein supporters made it clear that they were voting for these candidates because they believed in their policies and could not support either Clinton or Trump. But Libertarians who believe in free trade now have a president who does not, and Greens who want action on climate change now have a president who has called climate change a hoax.

A YouGov poll just before Election Day suggested that 26% of likely third-party voters preferred a Clinton presidency with a Republican-controlled Congress, while 12% preferred a Clinton presidency with a Democrat Congress. Only 17% said they preferred a Trump presidency. But the exit polls show that, if forced to choose between Clinton or Trump, about 25% of Johnson and Stein voters would have cast a ballot for Clinton, and about 15% would have chosen Trump. The remainder would not have voted. Under this formula, only one of these five states — Michigan — would have stayed with Clinton, but that would not have affected the final result.

Table 6.2 States won by Trump in which combined Libertarian and Green Party votes exceeded the margin between Trump and Clinton

State	Trump (%)	Clinton (%)	Margin	Libertarian vote	Green vote
Arizona	49.1	45.4	Trump +3.7	3.9	1.2
Florida	49.1	47.8	Trump +1.3	2.2	0.7
Michigan	47.6	47.3	Trump +0.3	3.6	1.1
Pennsylvania	48.8	47.6	Trump +1.2	2.4	0.8
Wisconsin	47.9	46.9	Trump +1.0	3.6	1.1

Gary Johnson, the former Republican governor of New Mexico, gained more than 5% of the vote in just 8 states (see Table 6.3), whilst Jill Stein's best result was a mere 3% in Hawaii. Another renegade Republican, Evan McMullin, ran as an independent in 11 states, winning just over 20% of the vote in his home state of New Mexico and just shy of 7% in Idaho. But the story of the 2016 election is that third parties in the United States are still more of a footnote than a phoenix.

Table 6.3 States in which Gary Johnson (Libertarian) won more than 5% of the vote

State	Vote for Gary Johnson (%)
New Mexico	9.3
North Dakota	6.3
Alaska	5.9
Oklahoma	5.7
Montana	5.6
South Dakota	5.6
Wyoming	5.3
Maine	5.1

It really was a close call

Those of us who forecast a Clinton victory had a nasty surprise coming in the small hours of that Wednesday morning. Watching CNN in our home in Dorset, I was keeping notes of how things were developing. At 2.20 a.m., UK time, just after the polls had closed in the Mountain Time Zone, I wrote a note to myself. It read simply, 'Trump could win'. But should I — not to mention all those dozens of polling organisations — feel foolish for getting it wrong? The head of a well-known polling organisation was asked during that evening, 'What did you get wrong?' Back came the simple answer: 'The numbers!'

But, in the end, the election was close. As we have just seen, it was close enough in some states to come down to the difference made by third-party candidates. And the *Washington Post* team published data a few days after the election showing that, out of the over 120 million votes cast, the election result was effectively decided by around 107,000 votes in three states. Had around 68,500 Trump voters in Pennsylvania, 11,500 Trump voters in Michigan, and 27,000 Trump voters in Wisconsin not cast their ballots, Clinton would have won those states' 46 Electoral votes, and with them the presidency. And those votes represent a mere 0.09% of the votes cast on 8 November. It was that close.

Typical Trump and Clinton voters

So what did typical Trump and Clinton voters look like? Two health warnings before answering that question. First, we are obviously making generalisations here and therefore these voter portraits need to be treated with some degree of caution. Second, with so many Americans in this election taking advantage of early voting, the exit polls from which these data are gleaned apply only to those who voted in person on Election Day itself. It's possible, of course, that in themselves they are not an accurate cross section of the 2016 electorate as a whole.

Table 6.4 Who voted for whom: 2012 and 2016 compared

Category (percentage in brackets)	2016		2012		Swing to Rep since 2012
	Trump (%)	Clinton (%)	Romney (%)	Obama (%)	
All (100%)	46.3	**48.0**	48	**51**	+2.2
Men (48)	**53**	41	**52**	45	+5
Women (52)	42	**54**	44	**55**	−1
Whites (70)	**58**	37	**59**	39	−1
African-Americans (12)	8	**88**	6	**93**	+7
Hispanics/Latinos (11)	29	**65**	27	**71**	+8
Asian (4)	29	**65**	26	**73**	+11
White men (34)	**63**	31	**62**	35	+5
White women (37)	**53**	43	**56**	42	+6
Black men (5)	13	**80**	11	**87**	+9

Table 6.4 Who voted for whom: 2012 and 2016 compared (contd.)

Category (percentage in brackets)	2016		2012		Swing to Rep since 2012
	Trump (%)	Clinton (%)	Romney (%)	Obama (%)	
Black women (7)	4	**94**	3	**96**	+3
Hispanic/Latino men (5)	33	**62**	33	**65**	+3
Hispanic/Latino women (6)	26	**68**	23	**76**	+11
Married (58)	**53**	43	**56**	42	−4
Non-married (42)	38	**55**	35	**62**	+2
Married men (29)	**58**	37	**60**	38	−1
Married women (30)	47	**49**	**53**	46	−9
Non-married men (19)	45	**46**	40	**56**	+15
Non-married women (23)	33	**62**	31	**67**	+7
Aged 18–29 (19)	37	**55**	37	**60**	+5
Aged 30–44 (25)	42	**50**	45	**52**	−1
Aged 45–64 (40)	**53**	44	**51**	47	+5
Aged 65+ (15)	**53**	45	**56**	44	+4
White 18–29	**48**	43	**51**	44	−2
White 30–44	**55**	37	**59**	38	+3
White 45–64	**63**	34	**61**	38	+6
White 65+	**58**	39	**61**	39	−3
High school graduate (18)	**51**	45	48	**51**	+9
Some college education (32)	**52**	43	48	**49**	+10
College graduate (32)	45	**49**	**51**	47	−8
Post-graduate (18)	37	**58**	42	**55**	−8
White non-college (34)	**67**	28	–	–	–
White non-college men	**72**	23	–	–	–
White non-college women	**62**	34	–	–	–
White college grad (37)	**49**	45	–	–	–
White college grad men	**54**	39	–	–	–
White college grad women	45	**51**	–	–	–
Population of area:					
City over 50,000 (34)	35	**59**	36	**62**	+2
Suburbs (49)	**50**	45	**59**	39	−15
Small town/rural (17)	**62**	34	**50**	48	+26
Democrats (37)	9	**89**	7	**92**	–
Republicans (33)	**90**	7	**93**	6	–
Independents (31)	**48**	42	**50**	45	–

Category (percentage in brackets)	2016		2012		Swing to Rep since 2012
	Trump (%)	Clinton (%)	Romney (%)	Obama (%)	
Liberal (26)	10	**84**	11	**86**	+1
Moderate (39)	41	**52**	41	**56**	+4
Conservative (35)	**81**	15	**82**	17	+1
Family income:					
Under $30,000 (17)	41	**53**	35	63	+16
$30K–49,999 (19)	42	**51**	42	57	+6
$50K–99,999 (31)	**50**	46	52	46	–2
$100K–199,999 (24)	**48**	47	54	44	–9
$200K and over (10)	**48**	47	54	44	–9

Winner in bold

But that having been said, the exit poll data (Table 6.4) give us a clear picture of the most significant voting trends of 2016 and how these had changed from four years previously. The typical Trump voter was therefore an older, white, married man with only a high school or some college education, living in a small town or rural area in the South or Midwest of America. On average, he was also poorer than his 2012 counterpart. The typical Clinton voter was a younger, ethnic, single woman with a college degree, living in a large city on the coastal fringes of America. On average, she was also less poor than her 2012 counterpart.

We can also see that Trump's big gains on Romney in 2012 were among five groups of voters: non-married men (a swing of 15 points); voters with only a high school education (+9 points) as well as those who had some college education (+10 points); voters living in small town and rural America (+26 points); and the poorest voters (+16 points). So how did Trump win the election, and specifically how did he significantly out-perform Mitt Romney amongst these key groups of voters? It is those questions that we shall address in the next chapter.

Questions
1 What is meant by 'the Blue Wall' and to what extent did Donald Trump pull it down?
2 What do the data in the fourth column of Table 6.1 tell us about the election results?
3 Did third parties play an important role in this election?
4 Which voting blocs were most important in their support of Trump?
5 How close was the final result?
6 What do typical Trump and Clinton voters look like?

Chapter 7

Why did Trump win?

Or why did Clinton lose?

Political operatives in the United States like to tell the story of a dog food company executive who complained that his product had the best ingredients, the best packaging and the lowest price, but the sales were still poor. Having assembled his employees and shareholders for their annual meeting, the boss asked the assembled group the simple question — 'Why?' From the back of the room came the reply: 'Dogs don't like it!'

The anecdote fits the Clinton campaign with embarrassing ease. Hillary Clinton had the best résumé of anyone who had run for president in recent memory: first lady, senator and secretary of state. Her campaign was disciplined and well financed. She had the name recognition, political experience, money-raising ability and organisational structure that most candidates would kill for. She had the respect and admiration of those who worked for her and — as she showed in her moving concession speech — many other qualities one looks for in a president. And she was running against the least-qualified, least-experienced and least-liked candidate that the nation had ever seen — a candidate who at times even seemed to be running against his own party. Indeed, she really did think that she had the best ingredients and the best (media) packaging. So how could she lose? Answer: the voters didn't like it.

It will be much debated for years to come whether this was an election that Trump won or that Clinton lost. Maybe it was a bit of both. We shall certainly find evidence of both. But, as is customary in this publication, we have asked the question from the point of view of the victor rather than the vanquished. Carl Cannon, the Washington bureau chief of the RealClearPolitics website, published an article two days after the election in which he offered 31 reasons why Trump won. Readers will be relieved to know that here we are rather more disciplined. So Box 7.1 gives five reasons why the impossible happened.

Box 7.1	Why Trump won: a summary

1 A coalition of resentments
2 The 'sneering liberal elites'
3 Out-of-touch Republican leadership
4 The Trump persona
5 Clinton's weak and flawed candidacy

Why did Trump win?

A coalition of resentments

All the way through the Republican primaries it was clear that Donald Trump was tapping into a vein of anger and resentment among certain groups of Republican voters. They were dissatisfied or even angry with the federal government. Put simply, they felt they were strangers in their own country. Indeed, they hardly recognised the America they now lived in compared with the one in which they were born and brought up. America had changed racially, economically, socially and morally, and many Americans resented these changes.

> ### Box 7.2 Things Americans were resentful about
>
> Many Americans were resentful about:
>
> - illegal immigration
> - globalisation
> - international trade deals
> - corporate greed
> - decaying communities
> - bank bailouts
> - political correctness
> - the advancement of 'marriage equality'
> - the election of a black president

America's cities and suburbs had become more racially diverse. When today's American seniors were born — mostly in the 1930s, 1940s and early 1950s — America was 90% white. By 1990, that figure had fallen to 80%, and in the election of 2016 the electorate would register as just 70% white. Even those who still lived in the white enclaves of America — mostly small towns or rural areas in the eastern half of the nation — knew that 'out there' America had changed, and some felt resentful. So they felt resentful at the levels of **immigration**, especially from Central America (Mexicans) and the Middle East (Muslims). And they felt very resentful about illegal immigrants. Then along came Donald Trump and railed against illegal immigrants — Mexicans and Muslims — and promised to deport them and build a wall along the USA–Mexico border. As Table 7.1 shows, exit polls found that one-quarter of voters supported the enforced deportation of illegal immigrants, and 84% of those voters supported Trump. And of the 41% of voters who said they supported the building of Trump's infamous wall along the Mexican border, 86% voted for Trump (see Table 7.2).

Table 7.1 Exit poll data on illegal immigrants

Illegal immigrants working in the United States should be:	Trump (%)	Clinton (%)
Offered legal status (70%)	34	60
Deported to home country (25%)	84	14

Table 7.2 Exit poll data on wall along Mexican border

View of the US wall along the entire Mexican border:	Trump (%)	Clinton (%)
Support (41%)	86	10
Oppose (57%)	17	76

And that wasn't all that had changed in their beloved America. Things had changed economically, and they believed the line that Trump pedalled that this was because of **globalisation** and **international trade agreements** that meant good American jobs went abroad — often to Mexico or Canada — helped along by the North American Free Trade Agreement (NAFTA), which was signed by Hillary's husband Bill when he was president, and the Trans-Pacific Partnership (TPP), which was signed by President Obama earlier in 2016. But Washington politicians — even many Republicans — had backed both NAFTA and TPP. Then along came Donald Trump, who called NAFTA 'the single worst trade deal — ever' and blamed Bill Clinton for signing it and Hillary for supporting it. And that was what decided Emmett Lawson — an African American who had lived in Cleveland, Ohio, until he lost his job in a steel mill and moved to Orlando, Florida — to switch from voting for Obama in 2012 to supporting Trump in 2016. Lawson, who now drives a lorry across Florida, told a *Los Angeles Times* reporter: 'NAFTA was bad, and Trump exploited it. He saw it and spoke out about it. That spoke to me. Trump is a business guy and that's the change that's needed.' Back in 1992, independent candidate Ross Perot had warned of 'a giant sucking sound' of jobs leaving the United States for Mexico if NAFTA was passed. Both the major party candidates in that year's election — Bill Clinton and President George H. W. Bush — along with top economists and media folk scoffed at Perot. But by 2016, both Bernie Sanders in the Democratic primaries and Donald Trump in the general election had realised the resentment that many Americans felt over such deals. As Table 7.3 shows, exit polls found that whereas 38% of Americans thought that international trade created jobs in the United States, 42% thought it took jobs away. And of that 42%, two-thirds voted for Trump.

Table 7.3 Exit poll data on international trade

Effect of international trade:	Trump (%)	Clinton (%)
Creates US jobs (38%)	35	59
Takes away US jobs (42%)	65	31
Does not affect US jobs (11%)	30	63

In February 2016, a US conglomerate called United Technologies (UT) abruptly announced it was closing two Indiana plants and moving them to Mexico. Both factories were profitable, but UT can pay workers far less in Mexico and then import the products back into the United States at no charge, thanks to NAFTA. The firm, which makes billions of dollars from government contracts, recently paid its departing CEO a $184 million severance package. Sanders and Trump both railed against **corporate greed** and won their respective party Indiana primaries in May, and Trump carried the state in November by 57% to 38% — a state that Obama had won in 2008.

In recent elections the now somewhat ageing American singer-songwriter Bruce Springsteen had loyally turned out to support Democratic candidates. He did his bit again this year, appearing at a huge get-out-the-vote rally in Philadelphia on the last night of the campaign, together with Bill and Hillary Clinton as well as Barack and Michelle Obama. He praised Hillary and tore into Trump before singing three songs. But one number he carefully avoided was his 1984 song 'My Hometown', with its lyrics:

> They're closing down the textile mill
> Across the railroad tracks.
> The foreman says these jobs are going, boys,
> And they ain't coming back — to your hometown.

And it was in **decaying communities** like these, which were slowly withering away, that Trump found his voice, and his message of 'Make America Great Again' resonated, especially with white, older, blue-collar workers — the descendants of the Reagan Democrats who had turned out for Ronald Reagan in vast numbers over three decades ago — in places like Erie County, Pennsylvania, and Wayne County, Iowa, or Monroe and Adams counties in Ohio (see Table 7.4).

Table 7.4 Voting in selected counties: 2012 and 2016 compared

State/county	2012 Romney–Obama	2016 Trump–Clinton	Swing to the Republicans
Pennsylvania			
Bradford County	61–37	83–15	+44
Wyoming County	55–43	67–29	+26
Elk County	57–41	70–26	+28
Iowa			
Taylor County	56–42	70–25	+31
Wayne County	55–43	71–25	+34
Davis County	57–41	71–25	+30
Wisconsin			
Oconto County	54–45	67–30	+28
Marinette County	51–48	65–31	+31
Ohio			
Belmont County	53–45	70–28	+34
Scioto County	50–48	68–30	+36
Monroe County	52–45	72–25	+40

Take Wayne County, for example, in south-central Iowa. Its population is 99% white, but 14% are below are the poverty level. It was home to nearly 12,000 people back in 1950. Now it numbers just over 6,000. In 2012, it voted 55%–43% for Romney over Obama, giving the Republicans a 12-point victory. In 2016, Trump had a 46-point victory margin over Clinton, with 71% of the vote to Clinton's 25%. It was the same story in Monroe County, Ohio, where Romney had won by 7 points in 2012, but now Trump won by 47 points.

When the economy went pear-shaped in 2008–09, many blue-collar Americans felt that they had been made to carry most of the resulting financial hardship. President Obama boasted about having saved America from going over the fiscal cliff and claimed credit for the recovery. But politicians of both parties underestimated the degree of anger and pain in the nation — the degree to which 'the recovery' had been only for a fortunate few, while many more experienced stagnation or decline. As the protest chant went, 'Banks got bailed out, we got sold out'.

Illegal immigration, globalisation, trade, corporate greed, their own decaying communities and **bank bailouts** all helped stoke the feelings of anger and resentment in many blue-collar and rural communities — especially those east of the Missouri and Mississippi rivers. But this coalition of resentment was fuelled by other fears and frustrations. When politicians of both parties spoke, their words were seen as being masked in **political correctness**. Trump was different. These people believed Trump 'told it the way it is', unvarnished by what they regarded merely as the latest fads about racist or sexist language. From the beginning of his campaign when Trump called Mexican immigrants 'rapists', his insensitive comments and racist asides horrified the elites, journalists, so-called opinion formers and party leaders, as well as the ethnic groups he was maligning. But Trump's supporters chose to see it another way. They said his lack of a politically correct filter showed that he was 'genuine' — and as Carl Cannon put it, 'that he has guts to say what others won't'. Indeed, they saw Trump as a walking rebuke to what they regarded as the oddball college campus speech codes by which people expressing what used to be regarded as 'traditional' views — over, for example, same-sex marriage — were either shouted down or excluded from campuses altogether. When the Republican Party hierarchy from George H. W. Bush to Mitt Romney announced their distaste and disapproval of Trump's language, it only deepened his supporters' commitment to him. They saw such criticism as a badge of honour for their man.

Table 7.5 Exit poll data on Supreme Court appointments

In your vote, were Supreme Court appointments:	Trump (%)	Clinton (%)
The most important factor (21%)	56	41
An important factor (48%)	47	48
A minor factor (14%)	41	50
Not a factor at all (14%)	39	55

Another reason why many voters in small-town and rural America felt resentful was over the advancement of gay and transgender rights in general, and specifically that of what had become known as **'marriage equality'**. Tonya Register, a 57-year-old Trump supporter living in the smart southeast Los Angeles suburb of Fountain Valley, told the *LA Times* that she had nothing against Mexicans or the Asian immigrants filling up her Orange County neighbourhood. But she did object to 'seeing the White House lit up in rainbow colours to celebrate the Supreme Court's legalisation of same-sex marriage' in June 2015. 'That was not cool to me,' she added, 'and I'm an American too.' This may be why the issue of Supreme Court appointments was so important for Trump voters (see Table 7.5). A stunning 21% told exit pollsters that appointments to the Supreme Court were the most important factor in determining their vote, and of them, 56% voted for Donald Trump and only 41% for Hillary Clinton. This is what we might call the 'Antonin Scalia effect'. Justice Scalia was a hero to these voters — a justice who in their eyes fought to keep America how it was rather than how liberals wanted it to be, often in the most robust and feisty way. They didn't want Hillary Clinton appointing Scalia's replacement.

Table 7.6 Exit poll data on President Obama

Opinion of Barack Obama as president:	Trump (%)	Clinton (%)
Approve (53%)	10	84
Disapprove (45%)	90	6

Finally, for some there was still the simmering issue of the election in 2008 of Obama as **America's first black president**. True, Obama was still relatively popular as he drew to the close of his second term, but of the 45% who disapproved of Obama, 90% voted for Trump (see Table 7.6). As David Remnick wrote in *The New Yorker* the day after the election:

> Barack Obama is popular, but racism did not die with America's first black president. Sexism is also alive and well. And for some Americans — and this is painful to admit — a woman following a black man to the White House was simply too much to swallow.

We have taken some time to lay out the coalition of resentments in detail because, without it, the next four factors might well not have followed. As David Brooks wrote in the *New York Times* on Election Day:

> The white working-class once sat comfortably at the core of the American idea, but now its members have seen their skills devalued, their neighbourhoods transformed, their family structures decimated and their dignity questioned. Marginalised, they commonly feel invisible, alienated and culturally pessimistic.

So they grabbed the levers of democracy and overthrew their political masters, taking over control of the Republican Party from the political elites. That might have been progress, even inspiring, except that the candidate they turned to was someone who toyed with bigotry, class hatred, misogyny and authoritarianism.

The 'sneering liberal elites'

First things first. What do we mean by an elite? An elite is a group of people who exercise major influence on, or control, the making of political, economic, cultural and social decisions. They tend to achieve their position of power through wealth, family status or supposed intellectual superiority. They constitute the 'power structure', the 'establishment', the 'movers and shakers', the 'ruling classes', the opinion formers. Thus one can identify the political elite (Washington), the financial elite (Wall Street), the intellectual elite (professors from Ivy League universities), the media elite (nationally syndicated columnists). By the 'liberal elite' is meant those who align themselves with the Democratic Party, or left-leaning media outlets such as the *New York Times* and the *Washington Post*. The allegation that they are 'sneering' at poorer, less well-educated Americans is of course a value judgement, but one that is widely held by the kinds of voters most supportive of Donald Trump in 2016.

Trump ran against the elites. Never mind that he was born rich, flaunted his wealth and lived like royalty in his New York penthouse. But, according to Marc Fisher, 'he defined this election as a people's uprising against all the institutions that had let them down and sneered at them — the politicians, the parties, the Washington establishment, the news media, Hollywood, academia, all of the affluent, highly-educated sectors of society that had done well'. Enough of elites, Trump told them. Enough of experts, enough of the status quo, enough of the liberal intelligentsia and the liberal media, the elites of the East and West coasts, enough of the financial elite who brought them the 2008 meltdown and stagnant incomes, and jobs disappearing off shore. And it was by spreading this message to a large enough audience who were receptive to it that states like Ohio, Wisconsin, Michigan and Pennsylvania lurched into the Trump column on Election Day. In the words of Roger Cohen ('President Donald Trump', *New York Times*, 9 November), Trump's victory was 'the revenge of Middle America, above all of a white working-class America, troubled by changing social and cultural norms', pointing out to America's liberal elite that 'not every American loves choose-your-gender toilets'. As Figure 7.1 shows, Republican support from white, non-college-educated voters at 67% was the highest in ten elections.

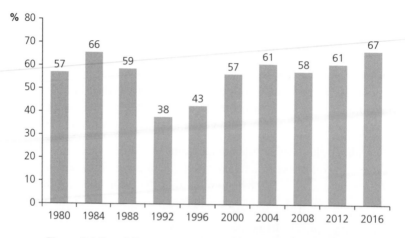

Figure 7.1 Republican support amongst white, non-college educated voters, 1980–2016

And if you want to know what the sneering elite sounds like, then Box 7.3 provides three classic examples taken from the last three presidential campaigns. It is comments like these that give the impression to those left behind by the American Dream that the nation's elites are looking down their noses at them, regarding them as buffoons or Rednecks, in what one commentator tellingly refers to as 'point-and-laugh liberalism'. It powerfully fuelled Donald Trump's campaign as he proclaimed himself the saviour of what he called 'the forgotten men and women of our country'.

Box 7.3 **Three presidential candidates denigrating the kinds of voters who would support Trump in 2016**

You go into these small towns in Pennsylvania, the jobs have gone now for 25 years and nothing's replaced them. So it's not surprising then that they get bitter, they cling to guns or religion or antipathy to other people who aren't like them as a way to explain their frustrations.

Barack Obama, addressing a fundraiser in San Francisco, April 2008

There are 47% who are with Obama, who are dependent on government, who believe they are victims, and who believe the government has a responsibility to care for them. These are people who pay no income tax, and so my job is not to worry about those people. I'll never convince them that they should take personal responsibility and care for their lives.

Mitt Romney, addressing a fundraiser in Boca Raton, Florida, May 2012

You know, just to be grossly generalistic, you could put half of Trump's supporters into what I call the basket of deplorables — the racist, sexist, homophobic, xenophobic, Islamophobic, you name it. And unfortunately there are people like that. And he has lifted them up. Now some of those folks, they are irredeemable, but thankfully, they are not America.

Hillary Clinton, addressing an LBGT rally in New York City, September 2016

Out-of-touch Republican leadership

Late in 2015, a number of manufacturing executives had gathered in Atlanta, Georgia, to honour their senior United States senator Johnny Isakson for his tireless efforts on their behalf in Washington. But as the lunch was winding down, Mr Isakson found himself facing a man from Coweta County, just southwest of Atlanta. The man, Burl Finkelstein, said that trade policies with Mexico and China were strangling the family-owned kitchen-parts company he helped manage, and threatening the jobs provided. Talking to a reporter in March 2016, Finkelstein recalled that Mr Isakson politely brushed him off, just as he had many times before. So Finkelstein voted for Donald Trump — 'he gets it'. But this is just one story of the Republican Party abandoning its most faithful voters, who had been facing economic pain and uncertainty over the past decade as the party's big donors, lawmakers and lobbyists had prospered. From mobile home parks in rural Florida, to Virginia's coal country, to factory towns in Michigan, disenchanted Republican voters lost faith in the agenda of their own party leaders.

We have already seen in Chapter 3 how Trump charted a different course compared with the Republican leadership (see Table 3.7). The fact that Trump was not really a Republican helped him too, in much the same way as the fact that Bernie Sanders was not really a Democrat helped him to run against his party establishment in the Democratic primaries. Since 1999, Trump had been a registered Democrat, an independent, a member of the Reform Party and finally a Republican. His own party establishment wrote him off as an opportunist, but it helped Trump with voters who had lost faith in their own party leadership. They had repudiated 14 conventional Republican politicians in the primaries and now Trump was able to appeal to his supporters despite the antagonism of much of the party leadership. For many Americans, Trump was a bomb they were willing to throw at the system they felt was failing them — and that included the Republican Party.

To briefly recap the story so far: we have shown that we had in 2016 a significant bloc of voters who felt neglected and resentful. More than that, they felt insulted and demeaned by the nation's liberal elite and betrayed by the leadership of their own party. Without all that in place, Donald Trump's campaign would have crash-landed on take-off, as it had done four years earlier. It's only with these first three factors in place that the Trump candidacy makes any sense at all, and that a Trump presidency becomes even a remote possibility.

The Trump persona

Forty years ago in the black comedy film *Network*, Peter Finch played Howard Beale, a TV anchorman who is going to be sacked because of declining ratings on his show. But in his last scheduled appearance, Beale makes a crazed and impassioned plea to his audience and to the nation.

> I don't have to tell you things are bad. Everybody knows they're bad. Everybody's out of work or scared of losing their job. Shopkeepers keep a gun under the counter. We sit watching our TVs while some local newscaster tells us that today we had 15 homicides and 63 violent crimes, as if that's the way it's supposed to be. Well, I want you to get mad. I don't know what to do about the inflation, and the Russians, and the crime in the street. All I know is first you've got to get mad. You've got to say, 'I'm a human-being. My life has value.'

It all sounds a bit like Trump's acceptance speech at the Republican convention, or Trump at a hundred and more rallies throughout the country during the campaign. But then Beale makes his memorable pitch.

> So I want you to get up now, all of you. Get up out of your chairs and go to the window, open it, and stick your head out and yell, 'I'm as mad as hell, and I'm not going to take this any more.'

And to everyone's surprise, that's exactly what they do. 'They're yelling in Atlanta! They're yelling in Baton Rouge!' And on 8 November, they were yelling in Iowa, they were yelling in Wisconsin, in Ohio, in Pennsylvania, in Michigan — even in Atlanta and Baton Rouge.

Table 7.7 Exit poll data on Donald Trump

	Trump (%)	Clinton (%)
Importance of the debates:		
Important (64%)	47	50
Not important (30%)	57	38
Opinion of Donald Trump:		
Favourable (38%)	95	4
Unfavourable (60%)	15	77
Is Donald Trump honest and trustworthy?		
Yes (33%)	94	5
No (63%)	18	71
Is Donald Trump qualified to be president?		
Yes (38%)	94	4
No (60%)	18	75
Does Donald Trump have the temperament to be president?		
Yes (35%)	94	5
No (63%)	20	72
Does Donald Trump's treatment of women bother you?		
Yes (70%)	29	65
No (29%)	87	9

Trump had spent decades cultivating an image of the guy who is so rich, so audacious, so unpredictable, that he would get done what ordinary politicians could not do. Whether it's anything more than an image, they and we are about to find out. 'I think he has such an ego, he couldn't stand to fail,' said Mary Vesley, 74, a Trump voter from Mechanicsville, Virginia, on Election Day. From the moment he rode down the escalator in Trump Tower in the summer of 2015, he presented himself as the antidote to the politicians and the elites. And he believed he would do it — even when, it seemed, no one else did. First he defeated 16 Republican opponents in the primaries. Like a playground bully, Trump taunted his opponents with just the right insult. The original front runner and brother of Obama's predecessor George W. Bush was 'Low energy Jeb'. The diminutive Senator Rubio from Florida was 'Little Marco'. And then in the general election it was 'Crooked Hillary'. For any politician, such behaviour would have disqualified them from the race. But for Trump the pop media icon, people thought it merely showed he was 'genuine'.

Trump lost all three presidential debates, but although 64% of voters said the debates were important in deciding their vote, of that 64%, 47% still voted for Trump (see Table 7.7). Of the staggering 60% of voters who had an unfavourable opinion of Trump, more than one in seven still voted for him. Of the 63% of voters who thought he was dishonest, more than one in five still voted for him. And it was much the same amongst the 60% of voters who thought he was unqualified to be

president, and the 63% who thought he lacked the temperament to be president. Trump even managed to get well over one-quarter of the votes of those who told pollsters they were bothered by Trump's treatment of women. Donald Trump really did seem to be the Teflon Candidate — the one to whom nothing stuck.

But whilst some saw something in his persona to admire, others saw something deeply troubling. David Brooks in the *New York Times* ('Let's Not Do This Again', 8 November) wrote of Trump's 'constant, flagrant and unapologetic lying, his penchant for cruelty, bigotry, narcissism, and selfishness', by which he 'shredded the accepted understandings of personal morality that prevent the strong from preying on the weak'. We know how Trump campaigned, but how will the Trump persona take to governing? From what we have seen thus far, the main problems could well be a short attention span, a short fuse, ignorance and incompetence. Will Trump be someone else who proves that the qualities needed to *become* president are not necessarily the same as those required to *be* president?

Clinton's weak and flawed candidacy

There will doubtless be much hand wringing within the Democratic Party following what must be the most surprising result in a presidential election since Harry Truman defeated Thomas Dewey in 1948. And the two questions that will doubtless receive a thousand answers are, first, could Hillary Clinton have done things differently and won, and secondly, could a different candidate have won?

There is much anecdotal evidence and some factual evidence that a significant number of 2012 Obama voters did not cast a ballot for Clinton in 2016. There could be three factors at play here. First, they could have voted but left the presidential portion of their ballot blank and voted only for down-ballot offices such as senator, congressman, governor, mayor and so on. Second, they could have switched their vote to either Trump or one of the third-party candidates. Or third, they could have stayed at home. Certainly at the time of writing it appears that, whereas the total Republican vote was up on 2012 — though not by a lot — the total Democrat vote was down, by possibly 1 million. Furthermore, as Figure 7.2 shows, Clinton's share of the popular vote was lower than that of either John Kerry in 2004 or Al Gore in 2000. True, Bill Clinton polled only 43% in 1992, but that was in an election in which independent candidate Ross Perot won 19%. So in terms of the popular vote percentage, this was really the Democrats' worst showing since Michael Dukakis in 1988.

Hillary Clinton has form on performing poorly in national elections. Back in 2008 she was surprisingly beaten in the Democratic primaries by an inexperienced, almost unknown senator who had less than four years' experience in national politics — Barack Obama. Then, as we saw in Chapter 2, earlier in 2016 she struggled to see off a 74-year-old senator from Vermont who was not even a paid-up member of the party — Bernie Sanders. This is hardly the record of a strong candidate.

In an election year in which voters were angry with the establishment and with professional politicians, Clinton was a candidate who could have been hand-

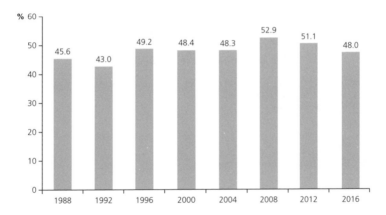

Figure 7.2 Democratic Party popular vote percentages, 1988–2016

picked by the Republicans just to make it easier for them to win. Clinton is a professional politician to her fingertips, having spent well over 30 years in state and national politics: 12 years as first lady of Arkansas; 8 years as first lady of the United States; 8 years as a United States senator from New York; 4 years as secretary of state. The Democratic primaries had shown her inability to engage with white, working-class voters — especially men. As a result, when she took big hits in rural areas, she could not make up for that in the cities. Turnout fell in heavily black cities like Philadelphia, Cleveland, Detroit and Milwaukee, all of which contributed to her losing Pennsylvania, Ohio, Michigan and Wisconsin to Trump. And, even more surprisingly, the expected surge among women and Hispanic voters, who had been so insulted by Trump, failed to materialise. Even with the allegations of sexual assault made against Trump by a dozen women, as well as his 'locker room talk' and the prospect of electing the first woman president, the Democrats' share of the vote among women fell from 55% in 2012 to 54%. Furthermore, against the candidate who had built his campaign round a pledge to build a wall along the Mexican border and make Mexico to pay for it, insulted a federal judge of Mexican descent, and described Mexicans as 'criminals' and 'rapists', Clinton's vote actually fell by 6 percentage points among Hispanics (from 71 to 65) from 2012.

Clinton was a weak candidate partly because she is such an uninspiring campaigner. The trouble with having the Obamas campaigning for her was that it merely emphasised how much better they were at working a crowd than she was. Who can forget Michelle Obama's 'when they go low, we go high'? But who can remember any line from a Clinton speech — other than the one about the 'basket of deplorables'? Neither did her campaign have any enthusing, over-arching theme to it. Most of the television ads she ran were more about painting Trump as a dangerous extremist, an outsider unfit for office, than pitching any plan of her own for change. And Clinton's answer to 'Making America Great Again' was 'Stronger Together' or 'I'm With Her' — not really slogans to inspire. As one commentator wrote, 'When your response to a cry of "Make America

Great Again!" is "America Is Already Great!" you'd better be sure that it feels true to a majority of voters, and the results show that it did not.'

Table 7.8 Exit poll data on Hillary Clinton

	Trump (%)	Clinton (%)
Opinion of Hillary Clinton:		
Favourable (44%)	3	95
Unfavourable (54%)	82	11
Is Hillary Clinton honest and trustworthy?		
Yes (36%)	4	94
No (61%)	73	20
Is Hillary Clinton qualified to be president?		
Yes (52%)	9	86
No (47%)	90	5
Does Hillary Clinton have the temperament to be president?		
Yes (55%)	13	82
No (43%)	89	5
Does Hillary Clinton's use of private e-mail bother you?		
Yes (63%)	70	24
No (36%)	6	90

In the aftermath of her defeat, Clinton seemed to suggest that the main reason why she lost was because of the action of FBI Director James Comey in reintroducing the issue of her use of a private e-mail server whilst serving as secretary of state less than a fortnight before Election Day. In a conference call with donors four days after the election, Mrs Clinton said: 'There are lots of reasons why an election like this is not successful, but our analysis is that Comey's letter raising doubts that were groundless, baseless, stopped our momentum.' Indeed, the action by Director Comey was, to say the least, unusual. And when he announced a week later that, after all, there was nothing new to report, his behaviour seemed highly questionable. Clinton claimed that this episode stopped her momentum in the final two weeks of the campaign and allowed Trump to talk louder and longer about 'Crooked Hillary'. The statistical evidence on this is, however, inconclusive. True, Trump did gain 2 percentage points in the polls between 28 October (the date of the first Comey announcement) and 6 November (the second announcement). But on the other hand, the slide in Clinton's numbers began ten days before Comey's first letter to Congress. She had already lost 2 percentage points in the polls between 18 and 28 October.

But although Clinton might have felt rightly aggrieved at Comey's behaviour, the problem went much deeper than that. If Clinton had not foolishly used her private e-mail server for state department business, if she had not equivocated time and again when the issue was brought to light, if she and her husband had not got caught up in all the somewhat sleazy-looking stories concerning the Clinton Foundation, if it hadn't looked as though she was saying one thing to Wall Street financiers (whilst being paid $500,000 per speech) and something else on the campaign trail, then 61% of voters would not have thought that she was dishonest and untrustworthy (see Table 7.8). And just short of three-quarters of those voters cast their ballots for Donald Trump. Neither could she entirely blame Mr Comey for the fact that 63% of voters were bothered about the whole e-mail server thing, and 70% of them voted for her opponent. Clinton had spent the entire year insisting that the whole e-mail business was a non-issue. It turned out she was wrong about that, and in the end she and Donald Trump exhibited what one might call 'a parity of sleaze'.

Table 7.9 Selected data from exit polls

	Trump (%)	Clinton (%)
Which candidate quality mattered most?		
Can bring change (39%)	83	14
Right experience (21%)	8	90
Good judgement (20%)	26	66
Cares about people like me (15%)	35	58
Direction of the country:		
Right direction (33%)	8	90
On the wrong track (62%)	69	25
Next president should:		
Continue Obama's policies (28%)	5	91
Be more conservative (48%)	83	13
Be more liberal (17%)	23	70

As Table 7.9 shows, in a country that wanted change, Hillary Clinton was the wrong candidate. In an election where the vast majority of voters thought the country was 'on the wrong track', Hillary Clinton, as someone so closely linked with the incumbent president, was the wrong candidate. For an electorate who wanted the country to be taken in a more conservative direction, she was the wrong candidate. The bottom row of Table 7.9 should also give pause for thought to those who have claimed that Bernie Sanders would have been a stronger candidate.

Finally, Clinton suffered from a passion gap. We saw this in 2008, and we saw it again in the primaries of 2016. Hillary Clinton is not a candidate who engenders genuine passion amongst many of her supporters. This brought to light a long-running problem for the Democrats — how to get out the vote in winning numbers when Barack Obama is not on the ballot himself. We saw this in the midterm elections in both 2010 and 2014. Now we know that the Obama factor turns out to be non-transferable, and when it came to another Clinton presidency, 'the dogs didn't like it!'

Conclusion

We have been saying for more than a decade now that America is a deeply divided nation. Its name — the *United* States of America — is something of an irony. According to David Brooks, 'this election campaign has been rather like a flash flood that sweeps away the topsoil and both reveals and widens the chasms'. We have seen that America is a more divided nation than ever we thought. We like to think of democracy as a conversation of ideas. What we have seen is a stream of shouted insults. Americans have retreated to their tribal bunkers. We have learnt that for the past eight years, one part of the nation have felt like strangers in their own country. Now they seem determined to reverse the tables. Red and Blue America seem ever more incomprehensible to each other, and the nation has chosen a president not renowned for either listening or healing. The moral and political health of the country is, I fear, in danger. And I pray that I am wrong.

Questions

1 What does the author mean by a 'coalition of resentments'? Who was resentful and what were they resentful about?
2 Explain the term 'point-and-laugh liberalism' and its link to the comments in Box 7.3.
3 Give an example of the way the Republican leadership had become out of touch with their voters.
4 What do the data in Table 7.7 tell us about Donald Trump and why people voted for him?
5 In what ways was Hillary Clinton a weak and flawed candidate?
6 What do the data in Table 7.9 tell us about 2016 being a difficult year for Clinton?
7 What does the author suggest is ironic about the title 'the United States of America'?

Chapter 8

The congressional elections: ending divided government?

Senate elections

Senators are elected to six-year terms with one-third being re-elected every two years. So in 2016 those 34 senators elected to office in 2010 were up for re-election. Twenty-four were Republicans and ten were Democrats. Five senators retired, thus creating open races in these states — California, Maryland and Nevada for the Democrats; Indiana and Louisiana for the Republicans. Unusually, all five open seats were held by the incumbent party.

Table 8.1 Results of Senate elections, 2016

State	Winner	Party	%	Opponent	Party	%
Alabama	**Richard Shelby**	R	64	Ron Crumpton	D	36
Alaska	**Lisa Murkowski**	R	44	Joe Miller	Lib	30
Arizona	**John McCain**	R	53	Rep. Ann Kirkpatrick	D	41
Arkansas	**John Boozman**	R	60	Conner Eldridge	D	36
California	Kamala Harris	D	63	Rep. Loretta Sanchez	D	37
Colorado	**Michael Bennet**	D	49	Darryl Glenn	R	45
Connecticut	**Dick Blumenthal**	D	63	Dan Carter	R	35
Florida	**Marco Rubio**	R	52	Rep. Patrick Murphy	D	44
Georgia	**Johnny Isakson**	R	55	Jim Barksdale	D	41
Hawaii	**Brian Shatz**	D	74	John Carroll	R	22
Idaho	**Mike Crapo**	R	66	Jerry Sturgill	D	28
Illinois	Rep. Tammy Duckworth	D	54	**Mark Kirk**	R	40
Indiana	Rep. Todd Young	R	52	Ex-Sen. Evan Bayh	D	42
Iowa	**Charles Grassley**	R	60	Patty Judge	D	36
Kansas	**Jerry Moran**	R	62	Patrick Wiesner	D	32
Kentucky	**Rand Paul**	R	57	Jim Gray	D	43
Louisiana	John Kennedy	R	61	Foster Campbell	D	39

Table 8.1 Results of Senate elections, 2016 (contd.)

State	Winner	Party	%	Opponent	Party	%
Maryland	Rep. Chris Van Hollen	D	60	Kathy Szeliga	R	36
Missouri	**Roy Blunt**	R	49	Jason Kander	D	46
Nevada	Catherine Cortez Masto	D	47	Rep. Joe Heck	R	45
New Hampshire	Gov. Maggie Hassan	D	48	**Kelly Ayotte**	R	48
New York	**Charles Schumer**	D	70	Wendy Long	R	27
North Carolina	**Richard Burr**	R	51	Deborah Ross	D	45
North Dakota	**John Hoeven**	R	79	Eliot Glassheim	D	17
Ohio	**Rob Portman**	R	58	Ex-Gov. Ted Strickland	D	37
Oklahoma	**James Lankford**	R	68	Mike Workman	D	25
Oregon	**Ron Wyden**	D	57	Mark Callahan	R	34
Pennsylvania	**Pat Toomey**	R	49	Katie McGinty	D	47
South Carolina	**Tim Scott**	R	61	Thomas Dixon	D	37
South Dakota	**John Thune**	R	72	Jay Williams	D	28
Utah	**Mike Lee**	R	68	Misty Snow	D	27
Vermont	**Patrick Leahy**	D	61	Scott Milne	R	33
Washington	**Patty Murray**	D	60	Chris Vance	R	40
Wisconsin	**Ron Johnson**	R	50	Ex-Sen. Russ Feingold	D	47

Incumbents in bold

Before the election, the party balance in the Senate was 54 Republicans and 44 Democrats, with two independents who usually vote with the Democrats making it effectively 54–46. Thus the Democrats had to win five seats to be the majority — four if the Clinton–Kaine ticket won and Vice President Tim Kaine could cast his vote to break a 50–50 tie. Forecasts running up to the election suggested they would achieve this.

But as in the presidential race, the Democrats came up short, making an overall gain of just two seats. They managed to defeat two Republican incumbents. In Illinois, Representative Tammy Duckworth defeated one-term Senator Mark Kirk by 54% to 40%. In New Hampshire, Governor Maggie Hassan defeated one-term Senator Kelly Ayotte by only around 1,000 votes out of the over 700,000 cast (see Table 8.1). Other vulnerable incumbents who were expected to go down to defeat — Richard Burr in North Carolina, Pat Toomey in Pennsylvania and Ron Johnson in Wisconsin — all won relatively comfortably, possibly helped over the winning line by a strong showing from Donald Trump.

Table 8.2 Votes for winning Republican Senate candidates and votes for Trump compared

State	Vote for Trump (%)	Vote for winning Republican Senate candidate (%)	Senator ran ahead of Trump by:
Alabama	63	64	+1
Alaska	53	44	−9
Arizona	49	53	+4
Arkansas	60.4	59.8	−0.6
Florida	49	52	+3
Georgia	51	55	+4
Idaho	59	66	+7
Indiana	57	52	−5
Iowa	52	60	+8
Kansas	57	62	+5
Kentucky	63	57	−6
Missouri	57	49	−8
North Carolina	50.5	51.1	+0.6
North Dakota	64	79	+15
Ohio	52	58	+6
Oklahoma	65	68	+3
Pennsylvania	48.8	48.9	+0.1
South Carolina	55	61	+6
South Dakota	61	72	+11
Utah	47	68	+21
Wisconsin	48	50	+2

Although in the immediate aftermath of the election, Donald Trump was credited with keeping the Senate with a Republican majority, of the 21 Republicans who won their Senate races on 8 November, 16 of them got more votes than Trump (see Table 8.2). In only five states — Alaska, Arkansas, Indiana, Kentucky and Missouri — did Trump out-poll a winning Republican senator (see Table 8.2). Indeed, some Republican senators outpolled Trump very significantly — notably Mike Lee (Utah), John Hoeven (North Dakota) and John Thune (South Dakota).

The year 2016 was also noteworthy in that all 34 Senate races were won by the same party as won the presidential race in that state. New Hampshire almost bucked the trend but in the end gave exceedingly narrow majorities to the Democrats in both the presidential and Senate races.

As a result of these elections, the number of women in the Senate rises to a record high of 21, comprising 16 Democrats and 5 Republicans. Two women senators retired and one was defeated, but four new women were elected: Kamala Harris

(California), Tammy Duckworth (Illinois), Catherine Cortez Masto (Nevada) and Maggie Hassan (New Hampshire). The number of African American senators also increased to a new high of three with the re-election of Tim Scott (South Carolina) and the election of Kamala Harris. They join Senator Cory Booker of New Jersey. Scott is the only Republican of the three. Catherine Cortez Masto becomes the first Latina member of the Senate.

Political control of the Senate will be critical for President Trump, especially in terms of confirmation of his executive and judicial appointments, not least as he seeks to fill the vacancy on the Supreme Court left by the death of Justice Antonin Scalia in February 2016.

House elections

All 435 members of the House of Representatives are elected every two years. Before the election, the party balance in the House was 247 Republicans and 188 Democrats. Thus the Democrats had to make an overall gain of 30 seats to put them in the majority. Although they were never realistically going to make gains on that scale, they had hoped to gain between 10 and 15 seats and thereby make substantial inroads into the Republican 59-seat majority.

Table 8.3 Congressional District gains by party in House elections, 2016

Republican gains	Democrat gains
Florida 2	Florida 7
Florida 18	Florida 10
Nebraska 2	Florida 13
	Illinois 10
	New Hampshire 1
	New Jersey 5
	Nevada 3
	Nevada 4
	Virginia 4

But as Table 8.3 shows, the Democrats won 9 seats but lost 3, giving them an expected overall gain of just 6 seats and making the party balance in the new Congress 241–194 to the Republicans.

The end of divided government?

Like George W. Bush in 2001 and Barack Obama in 2009, Donald Trump will begin his presidency with his party in the majority in both houses of Congress. But Bush lost his majority in the Senate after just a few months when a Republican senator switched to become an independent, changing the Senate from a 50–50 split with Vice President Cheney controlling the casting vote to a 50–49 majority for the Democrats. If Trump enjoys Republican majorities in both houses of Congress for the first two years of his presidency, he will be first Republican president to do so since Dwight Eisenhower in 1953–54. If he enjoys it throughout his first term, then he will break a record going back to William McKinley at the end of the nineteenth century.

So although the 2016 elections have on paper ended divided government in Washington — at least for the time being — what will happen in practice? Will a Republican president and a Republican-controlled Congress work together productively in legislative harmony, or will the anti-establishment, bomb-throwing Trump version of Republican policies clash with the policy preferences of the 'establishment Republicans' in Congress? Will President Trump be able to develop a good working relationship with Republican House Speaker Paul Ryan? And how will the lugubrious Republican majority leader in the Senate, Mitch McConnell, fit in? Following a year of surprises, nothing seems very certain any more.

Questions

1 How has the make-up of the Senate been changed in terms of party balance, gender and race by the 2016 elections?
2 What was the overall change in seats by party in the House in the 2016 elections?
3 What possible problems might emerge between President Trump and the Republicans in Congress?

Chapter 9

The Supreme Court in 2016

What you need to know

- The Supreme Court is the highest federal court in the USA.
- The Court is made up of nine justices, appointed by the president, for life.
- Following the death in office of Justice Antonin Scalia in 2016, of the remaining eight justices, four were appointed by Republican presidents and four by Democrats.
- The Supreme Court has the power of judicial review. This is the power to declare acts of Congress or actions of the executive branch — or acts or actions of state governments — unconstitutional, and thereby null and void.
- By this power of judicial review, the Court acts as the umpire of the Constitution and plays a leading role in safeguarding Americans' rights and liberties.

The Supreme Court term that ended in June 2016 will probably be remembered more for it being an eight-person Court for its final four months than for the decisions it reached — or, as a result of tied votes, failed to reach. With the sudden death of Justice Antonin Scalia in mid-February and the impasse between President Obama and the Republican-controlled Senate resulting in a prolonged vacancy, the Court was down to just eight members as it rolled out its landmark decision in June. It was also significant that the Court had lost one of its most reliable conservative votes, thereby reducing the Court's conservative quartet to a conservative trio consisting of Chief Justice John Roberts with justices Clarence Thomas and Samuel Alito. From the other perspective, it put the Court's liberal quartet of justices Ruth Bader Ginsburg, Stephen Breyer, Sonia Sotomayor and Elena Kagan more in control of the nation's highest court. It was also thought that it could diminish the significance of the role of the so-called swing justice, Anthony Kennedy.

Table 9.1 Significant Supreme Court decisions, 2015–16 term

Case	Concerning	Decision
Fisher v. *University of Texas*	Affirmative action	4–3
Whole Woman's Health v. *Hellerstedt*	Abortion	5–3
United States v. *Texas*	Immigration	4–4

During the 2015–16 term, the Court handed down three landmark decisions — on affirmative action, immigration and abortion (Table 9.1). In this chapter we shall consider each in turn.

The Court and affirmative action

Abigail Fisher, a young woman from Texas, applied to the University of Texas but was rejected. Fisher, who is white, then filed a lawsuit arguing that she had been a victim of racial discrimination because minority race students with less impressive qualifications than hers had been accepted. Now here's a case not only of judicial review but of judicial *déjà vu*. The Supreme Court ruled on *Fisher v. University of Texas* in 2013 (see *US Government & Politics Annual Update 2014*, pp. 18–19). In a 7–1 decision the Court ruled that the university's use of race in its admissions policy must meet a test known as '**strict scrutiny**'. In his majority opinion back in 2013, Justice Kennedy stated that the lower courts had failed to apply such scrutiny. The federal appeal court was therefore instructed to rehear the case using the stricter scrutiny. That decision seemed to imply that a majority of the Supreme Court was sceptical that the university's admissions policy would survive such scrutiny. After all, Justice Ginsburg was the only justice to dissent and say that the appeal court's upholding of the university's admissions policy was constitutional. In July 2014, the appeal court reheard the case and again found in favour of the University of Texas, and Ms Fisher again appealed the decision to the Supreme Court. The expectation was therefore that a majority of the Supreme Court would strike down the appeal court's ruling and uphold Ms Fisher's claim of racial discrimination, thereby delivering a severe blow to this **affirmative action** programme.

> **Strict scrutiny** requires that, for a race-based recruitment programme to be used, all available and workable race-neutral alternatives do not work to achieve the desired goal of increasing racial diversity.
>
> **Affirmative action** is a programme that entails giving members of a previously disadvantaged minority group a head-start in such areas as higher education and employment.

But the Court did no such thing. In a 4–3 ruling — Justice Kagan took no part, having already been involved while serving as Solicitor General before joining the Court — the Court upheld the appeal court ruling, thereby also upholding the university's affirmative action programme. What was also a big surprise was that the majority opinion was written by Justice Kennedy, who has been a long-term sceptic of race-based admissions programmes and indeed had never voted to uphold any affirmative action plan. Was this yet another example of what some see as Kennedy, the unprincipled justice, who will merely say anything in order to be in the majority?

Here's what Justice Kennedy, joined by liberal justices Ruth Bader Ginsburg, Stephen Breyer and Sonia Sotomayor, had to say:

> A university is in large part defined by those 'intangible qualities which are incapable of objective measurement but which make for greatness'. Considerable deference is owed to a university in defining those intangible characteristics, like student body diversity, that are central to its identity and

educational mission. But still it remains an enduring challenge to our nation's education system to reconcile the pursuit of diversity with the constitutional promise of equal treatment and dignity.

It was the kind of rather grandiose waffle in which some think that Justice Kennedy specialises. With Kennedy, it's not so much the decisions he arrives at that are open to criticism as *the way* in which he arrives at them.

In his dissenting opinion, Justice Alito — joined by John Roberts and Clarence Thomas — called this 'affirmative action gone berserk based on offensive and unsupported stereotypes'. He went on: 'The majority's uncritical deference to the University of Texas's self-serving claims blatantly contradicts our decision in the prior judgement of this very case. Something very strange has happened since our prior decision.' According to Justice Alito:

> Even though the University of Texas has never produced any coherent explanation for its asserted need to discriminate on the basis of race, and even though the University of Texas's position relies on a series of unsupported and noxious racial assumptions, the majority concludes that the university has met its heavy burden. This conclusion is remarkable — and remarkably wrong.

Reactions to the decision were varied. President Obama led the praise of the Court's ruling, saying that the Court had 'upheld the basic notion that [racial] diversity is an important value in our society and that this country should provide a high-quality education for all our young people, regardless of their background'. Of course, the irony is that Ms Fisher would agree with that, and here lies the great conundrum of affirmative action — that ending racial discrimination is brought about by...racial discrimination! Laurence Tribe, a law professor at Harvard, surpassed even the president's eulogy by claiming that 'no decision since *Brown* v. *Board of Education* in 1954 has been as important as *Fisher* will prove to be in the long history of racial inclusion and educational diversity'. On the other hand, critics of the decision, such as Roger Clegg of the Center for Equal Opportunity, which supports 'colour-blind' policies, believed that the decision 'leaves plenty of room for future challenges to racial preference policies at other schools — the struggle goes on'.

The Court and abortion

Anthony Kennedy was on another philosophical walk-about in the Court's landmark decision on abortion. In his nearly 30 years on the highest court, Justice Kennedy had only once found an abortion restriction unconstitutional, and that was back in 1992 in *Planned Parenthood* v. *Casey*. Twenty-four years later, in 2016, he found another. This case was also based in Texas and concerned two parts of a law that imposed strict requirements on abortion providers in the state, signed into law in July 2013 by the then governor, Rick Perry. One restriction required all abortion clinics in the state to meet the standards of what Americans call an ambulatory surgical centre — a medical facility that offers procedures that are too complicated for a doctor's surgery but do not require in-patient, overnight care. Another required doctors performing abortions to have direct access to in-patient facilities at a nearby hospital.

In his majority decision in *Whole Woman's Health* v. *Hellerstedt,* Justice Breyer concluded that 'neither of these provisions offers medical benefits sufficient to justify the burdens upon access [to abortion services] that each imposes'. He continued: 'Each places a substantial obstacle in the path of women seeking an abortion, each constitutes an undue burden on abortion access, and each violates the Constitution.' Breyer was joined by justices Kennedy, Ginsburg, Sotomayor and Kagan. Chief Justice Roberts along with justices Thomas and Alito dissented. But it was Justice Kennedy's vote that was the critical one. Had Kennedy voted the other way, resulting in a 4–4 tie, the decision of the appeal court that had taken the contrary view and upheld the Texas law would have prevailed. David Cohen, a law professor at Drexel University in Philadelphia, described Kennedy's vote in this case as 'a puzzle', adding that 'he may have been swayed by the burdens placed on women having to drive hundreds of miles to have an abortion, or by the lack of medical evidence justifying the restrictions — or both'. Or, of course, Justice Kennedy may not be able to see a potential majority that he doesn't want to join.

President Obama was pleased with the Court's decision, tweeting, 'Pleased to see the Supreme Court reaffirm every woman has a constitutional right to make her own reproductive choices.' But Texas Attorney General Ken Paxton ridiculed the Supreme Court for its decision, commenting that 'the Court is becoming a default medical board for the nation, with no deference being given to state law'.

The Court and immigration
President Obama might have been very pleased with two of the Court's landmark decisions in its 2015 term, but he certainly was not pleased about the third — although had Justice Scalia still been alive, it could have been even worse.

Congress having failed to deliver any meaningful immigration reform legislation, in November 2014 President Obama issued an executive order — the Deferred Action for Parents of Americans and Lawful Permanent Residents (DAPA) — to allow certain illegal immigrants to be granted 'deferred action status', which means that although not granted full citizenship they would be subject to an indefinite delay in their deportation from the United States. To be eligible for DAPA, a person must:
- have lived in the United States without interruption since 1 January 2010
- be physically present in the United States when applying
- have a child who is a US citizen or lawful permanent resident
- be free from any criminal conviction
- not pose a threat to national security

This would have allowed some 5 million unauthorised immigrants who were parents of lawful residents legally to remain in the country.

In December of the same year, Texas along with 25 other states, all with Republican governors, challenged the president's action in federal court, calling it 'one of the largest changes in immigration policy in our nation's history', and claiming the president could not carry out such a programme without Congress's approval. In November 2015, the federal appeals court found against President Obama, stating that he did not have such powers, and that his action was unconstitutional as it breached the clause of Article II of the Constitution that requires the president to 'take care that the laws be faithfully executed'. The Justice Department announced it was asking the Supreme Court to review this decision.

The 4–4 tied decision left in place the federal appeals court decision blocking the plan. The Supreme Court's judgement amounted to just nine words: 'The judgement is affirmed by an equally divided court.' But such brevity masks the enormity of the decision. Walter Dellinger, a Clinton administration lawyer, commented: 'Seldom have the hopes of so many been crushed by so few words.' The President was distraught, stating:

> Today's decision is frustrating to those who seek to grow our economy and bring rationality to our immigration system. It is heartbreaking for the millions of immigrants who have made their lives here.

But Texas Attorney General Ken Paxton was delighted with the outcome, stating:

> Today's decision keeps in place what we have maintained from the start: one person, even a president, cannot unilaterally change the law. This is a major setback to President Obama's attempts to expand executive power, and a victory for those who believe in the separation of powers and the rule of law.

The brief judgement did not disclose how the justices voted, but they undoubtedly split along ideological lines, with the conservatives (Roberts, Thomas and Alito) plus Kennedy on one side, and the liberals (Ginsburg, Breyer, Sotomayor and Kagan) on the other. The President's side had optimistically hoped that Chief Justice Roberts might join his four more liberal colleagues and save the programme, as he had done over Obamacare. Robert Barnes, writing in the *Washington Post*, described President Obama as having 'suffered the biggest legal defeat of his administration'.

A summary of the 2015–16 term

The Court's ideological shift

The Court delivered 76 decisions in this term, very much par for the course as Table 9.2 shows. But that was just about the only thing that was 'average' about this year for the Court. Everything about this term changed in the early hours of 13 February as news emerged of the sudden death of Justice Antonin Scalia. This was a game changer. The Court had opened back in October with Scalia and his fellow conservatives in high hopes of a successful year. Their five-member grouping could hope to deliver in three big areas — affirmative action, abortion and immigration. But after Scalia's death and then Justice Kennedy's liberal conversion, this was the right-wing Court that suddenly evaporated.

Table 9.2 Total, unanimous and 5–4 decisions, 2010–16

Term:	2010–11	2011–12	2012–13	2013–14	2014–15	2015–16
Number of decisions	80	75	78	72	75	76
% which were unanimous	48	44	49	65	40	**50**
% which were 5–4 decisions	20	20	29	14	26	**5**

Table 9.2 also shows that the Court exhibited a high level of unanimity, but that 5–4 decisions were in very short supply. Whereas, in the previous year, a quarter of the Court's decision had been decided by just one vote, in this year only four of the 76 decisions fell into that category, which, because of the eight-member Court for most of the term, included cases decided by 4 votes to 3 as well as by 5 votes to 3. But two of these four narrow decisions were landmark decisions.

As in the previous term, the conservative group on the Court did poorly in these narrow decisions (see Table 9.3). Indeed, they won only one of the four narrow decisions, with the liberal quartet joined by Justice Kennedy winning the other three, including the two landmark judgements. So, as Adam Liptak observed in the *New York Times* ('The Right-Wing Supreme Court That Wasn't', 28 June 2016), 'for the second term in a row, the Court led by Chief Justice John Roberts delivered liberal decisions at a rate not seen since the famously liberal court led by Chief Justice Earl Warren in the 1950s and 1960s'.

Table 9.3 Percentage of conservative victories in 5–4 decisions

Term	Percentage of conservative victories in 5–4 decisions
2005–06	45
2006–07	54
2007–08	33
2008–09	48
2009–10	50
2010–11	63
2011–12	33
2012–13	43
2013–14	40
2014–15	26
2015–16	**25**

The effect of Scalia's death

Before this term began, the Court had agreed to hear a number of cases that conservative interest groups hoped would advance their agendas — on, for example, affirmative action, abortion and the environment. Just the month

before Scalia's death, the Court heard oral argument in *Friedrichs* v. *California Teachers' Association*. The case concerned whether teachers could be required to opt *out* of union dues being automatically deducted from their salaries: in other words, the money would be given to the union unless they objected. The plaintiff claimed this violated their First Amendment rights, and that people should be required to opt in: in other words, the money would go to the union only if the individual gave their actual consent. When the case was argued, the Court's conservative quartet — including Scalia — seemed ready to say that the 'opt out' option was indeed unconstitutional. At the justices' conference, Chief Justice Roberts assigned the writing of the majority opinion to fellow-conservative Justice Alito. But in March, the month after Scalia died, the Court announced that it was deadlocked in the case. The previous judgement — allowing the 'opt out' option — was left standing.

There was deadlock too, as we saw, in the Obama immigration case. But had Scalia still been alive, the decision would have been a lot worse for the president. Rather than issuing a nine-word statement, a Court including Scalia as a fifth vote to overturn Obama's executive order would have issued a lengthy and comprehensive rebuke to what Republicans say was a pattern of unconstitutional executive overreach by President Obama.

By the time the next president is inaugurated, Justice Breyer will be 78, Justice Kennedy will be 80, and Justice Ginsburg will be 83. Along with the Scalia vacancy, the new president could have the opportunity to reshape the Court for the next few decades, with two, three or maybe even four appointments to make. The Roberts Court seems certain to enter an entirely new phase, and it could be very different from the one presided over by the Chief Justice in his first decade.

Questions

1 Why was the decision in *Fisher* v. *University of Texas* such a surprise? Explain the role played by Justice Kennedy.
2 Were women's rights on abortion protected or further restricted by the Court's decision in the *Hellerstedt* decision? Explain your answer.
3 How did a nine-word decision in the *United States* v. *Texas* case present 'a major setback' to President Obama's immigration policy?
4 What effect did the sudden death of Justice Scalia have on the Supreme Court in 2016?
5 What further appointment opportunities to the Supreme Court may open up for the new president from 2017?